THE CULTURED CHEF

AN INTERNATIONAL GUIDE FOR KIDS WHO LOVE TO COOK

Written by Nico Seabright
Illustrated by Coleen McIntyre

Contributing Editor, Rachelle Matheson
Contributing Illustrator, Bianca Stancu

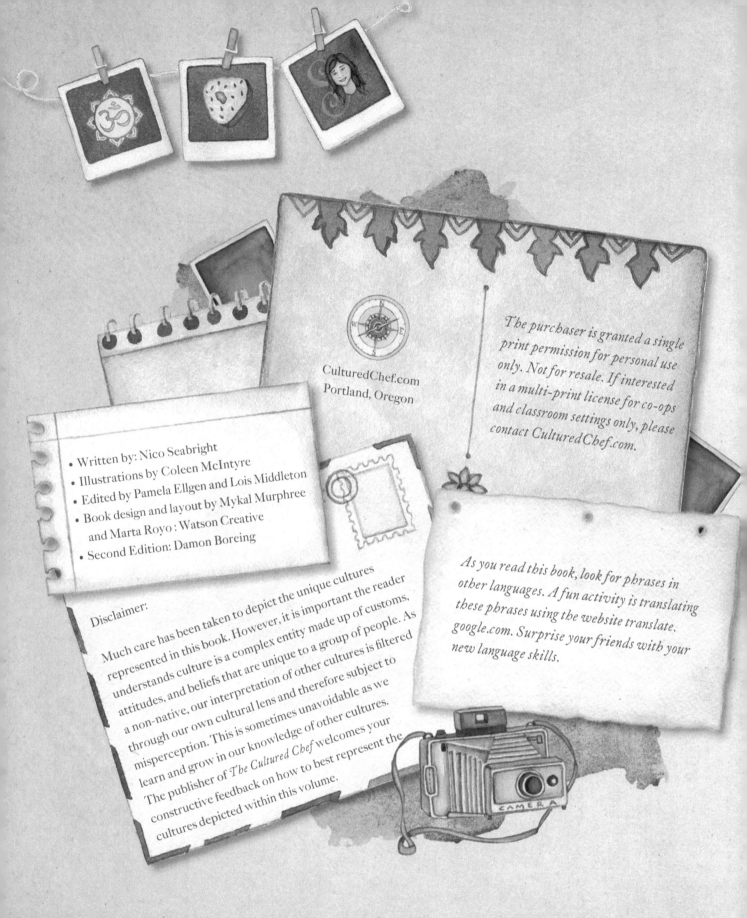

CulturedChef.com
Portland, Oregon

- Written by: Nico Seabright
- Illustrations by Coleen McIntyre
- Edited by Pamela Ellgen and Lois Middleton
- Book design and layout by Mykal Murphree and Marta Royo : Watson Creative
- Second Edition: Damon Boreing

Disclaimer:

Much care has been taken to depict the unique cultures represented in this book. However, it is important the reader understands culture is a complex entity made up of customs, attitudes, and beliefs that are unique to a group of people. As a non-native, our interpretation of other cultures is filtered through our own cultural lens and therefore subject to misperception. This is sometimes unavoidable as we learn and grow in our knowledge of other cultures. The publisher of *The Cultured Chef* welcomes your constructive feedback on how to best represent the cultures depicted within this volume.

As you read this book, look for phrases in other languages. A fun activity is translating these phrases using the website translate. google.com. Surprise your friends with your new language skills.

FOREWORD

Food and the Global Classroom

This beautiful and fascinating book by Nico Seabright is not only about food, but also the idea of global citizenship. This idea perhaps stretches back to Socrates, who allegedly said, "I am a citizen, not of Athens or Greece, but of the world." One way to create a cosmopolitan mindset -with a sense of empathy towards others- is to teach children using what unites us all, our love of food.

Every section is organized around a world region, with recipes and information from a few countries. For example, the section on Hawaii describes how to make Musubi rice balls (which entails a discussion of Hawaii's multicultural history), contains a kids' activity to make a Lei, and tells about the Hawaiian Naupaka legend. The section on Mexico describes Day of the Dead bread, and discusses the artwork of Frida Kahlo and Jose Guadelupe Posada. Nico Seabright does an excellent job concisely telling folk tales. Because one of the key goals of the book is to introduce children to global cultures, the work has unexpected sections such as "Musical Instruments of the World." Of course, not all nations have states, so this book also talks about the cuisine of the Choctaw in the United States, and the Inuit in Canada.

Most importantly, this book is meant to make kids excited to cook, so it includes many appealing recipes that children can make. It's hard to read the book and not want to cook Brazilian cheese bread or steak chimichurri pasta from Argentina.

Illustrator Coleen McIntyre has a gift for the use of color. The plates at the opening and close of the work shimmer with avocado green and rose colored tomatoes. Every page is filled with endless images of folklore, architecture, masks, animals and food. How did she find the time to create so many wonderful watercolors? Some of the illustrations -such as that which accompanies the Inuit folktale "Sky Full of Stories"- belong in an art gallery.

This cookbook is a wonderful resource for teachers in classes from kindergarten through grade school, particularly in International Schools, or schools with a global commitment. But it's also such a fun book that I think that many adults will have trouble putting it down. Enjoy.

Shawn Smallman, Professor
Department of International and Global Studies
Portland State University

Table of Contents

The Cultured Chef is dedicated to all of the dreamers who want to make discovering other cultures a way of life. You open your hearts and minds to building bridges instead of walls, and that is the first step toward beginning any adventure worth having.

INTRODUCTION

I want to personally thank you for your interest in **The Cultured Chef**. The book originally started as a conversation between a group of friends in a youth hostel in Central America, and eventually turned into the published work you are reading today. Through my travels I came to realize that food is an ideal medium for engaging a diverse audience in conversations about world culture. Mealtime is one of the primary activities that most humans have in common, and the ritual of preparing and consuming food becomes a big part of our personalities and cultural identity.

When I started working on **The Cultured Chef**, the goal was to channel my love of world culture, literature and the communal nature of food to help bridge the cultural divide that exists in many communities in the United States. I feel that if a child has positive multicultural experiences while they are young, their expanded worldview will help them grow into more compassionate and socially-engaged adults.

My hope is to create a book that not only educates, but also inspires young people to develop a global perspective and a new way of life. I truly believe this is the key to success for future generations. So let's band together and discover all the world has to offer.

Nico Seabright
Author, *The Cultured Chef*

We're offering a treasure trove of free resources on our website www.CulturedChef.com. You'll find audio stories, lesson plans and much more. Our hope is The Cultured Chef will help you explore and grow in a new worldview.

HOW TO BECOME A GLOBAL CITIZEN

What does it mean to be a global citizen? We live in a world that is becoming increasingly interconnected. Through technology, improvements in international travel options and exciting communication tools, such as Google Translate and Facebook, the world is becoming a much smaller place. Now it is possible to conduct business, make new friends and help others through global philanthropy with the simple click of a mouse.

Why Become a Global Citizen?

Learning about other cultures helps you become a well-rounded person, improving your ability to communicate better, meet new friends and get a better job. The more you study about the world you'll realize there are others who may be less fortunate than you. You can find ways to improve their lives through politics, philanthropy and volunteer efforts.

5 Ways to Become More Globally Aware

1. Develop an interest in how others do things differently around the world.
2. Read books, watch movies and listen to music from or about other countries.
3. Be open to experiencing new things. Try your hand at making art, music and food like they do in other cultures
4. Find out who is in need and how you can help. It doesn't matter whether you find the need in your own neighborhood or halfway around the world — simple things you do can make a huge difference in the lives of others.
5. Inspire future travel by learning about the culture, history and geography of places around the world.

What is Philanthropy?

Philanthropy begins when you realize that there are people in the world whose basic needs of food, clothing, shelter and education are not being met. It involves giving to an organization or individual who is actively helping to meet those needs or giving directly to the person in need. Giving can take many forms, whether you donate things you already own, your money or your time.

Here Are Some Ways You Can Start Making A Difference

Donate toys, school supplies and clothes to an orphanage or local shelter.

Make fun crafts or handmade books and deliver them to a retirement center.

Volunteer with your parents to do yard work for a senior in your neighborhood.

Volunteer at a soup kitchen or coordinate a canned food drive.

Visit Kiva.org and learn about micro-lending.

Introduce yourself to someone new at school and help make them feel special.

Hold a bake sale or carwash to raise money for someone in need.

Adopt an animal from a shelter or rescue facility.

Look for volunteer opportunities within your school, church or community.

Make ethical purchasing decisions and buy organic foods and fair trade goods whenever possible.

Learn a Foreign Language

Learning a foreign language allows us to better communicate with our friends and neighbors. High schools in the United States require students study a foreign language, but many students don't enjoy the experience. What about you? Why not try to make learning a foreign language fun? Many phrasebooks and games are available to help make learning a new language enjoyable.

WORLD TRAVELER'S GUIDE TO SUCCESS IN THE KITCHEN

With so many ingredients and complicated instructions, cooking can be a little confusing. But it doesn't have to be, especially if you learn a few of the basics first. This list of tips will help you be more organized, and will keep you safe as you prepare great tasting recipes in the kitchen with your friends and family.

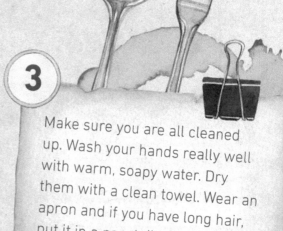

1 Make sure you don't have anything else going on. You need to focus on cooking right now. Be sure you have plenty of time to do all the things the recipe says.

3 Make sure you are all cleaned up. Wash your hands really well with warm, soapy water. Dry them with a clean towel. Wear an apron and if you have long hair, put it in a ponytail.

2 Read every single word of the recipe so you know all of the things you are supposed to have, both the ingredients and what kitchen tools you'll need to do the cooking. The recipe will also tell you what you are supposed to do in what order.

4 Keep cleaning! People are going to eat this stuff! Wipe off your counters, wash your baking dishes, measuring cups and spoons and the food you are going to cook.

5

Set out everything you will need to make the recipe, all the ingredients and all the equipment from your kitchen.

8

Double-check the glossary to make sure you understand what all the words in the recipe mean. You want to use the right measuring cups for certain ingredients. And you want to make sure you do exactly what the recipe is telling you.

6

If you are baking something, make sure you preheat the oven before you get started. Otherwise, you're going to have to hang around and wait for the oven to get hot after everything is all put together. That might wreck the food you are trying to prepare.

9

Be sure a grownup helps you in the kitchen. You might have to work with sharp knives and super hot ovens or burners. These are the things the adult should be doing with you or for you.

7

Measure out all of your ingredients before you start mixing it all together and cooking. Line them up on the counter leaving plenty of room for your workspace.

10

It is always a good idea to clean up as you work. If you have everything together before you start, you can stay on top of each task. Put used utensils in a sink of soapy water or in the dishwasher as you finish. It is a lot more fun to cook if you do not have to clean up a really big mess when you are all done!

COOKING GLOSSARY

Al Dente:
This is an Italian phrase that describes a way to cook pasta so it is tender but still a little firm.

De-bone:
Taking the meat off of the bones.

Beat:
Stirring really fast so you can add air into whatever you're mixing. Beating makes your mixture lighter and fluffier.

Dice:
Cutting into very small pieces about 1/8 to ¼ inch.

Blend:
Completely combine ingredients until everything is all mixed up and very smooth.

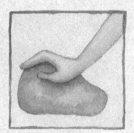

Knead:
Working the dough. Do this by folding and pressing dough together with the heels of your hands. Turn the pressed dough around by one quarter turn each time.

Coat:
Covering a food up with a layer of another ingredient, like dipping a strawberry in chocolate.

Marinate:
Soaking food in a sauce. Usually it is meat or vegetables. Place the food in a dish or bowl and pour the sauce over the top to cover it.

Combine:
Stirring together two or more ingredients until they are blended.

Mince:
Chopping into very fine pieces — smaller than a dice.

Cut In:
Mixing the solid fat into dry ingredients until they are all the same size pieces.

Mix:
Stirring until everything is blended together.

COOKING GLOSSARY

Preheat:
Turning on the oven ahead of time to make sure it is at the right temperature when it is time to cook the food.

Stir:
Mixing up ingredients with a spoon in big, slow circles so you don't beat in any air.

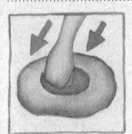

Punch-down:
Pushing down the puffed up dough with your fist. This makes the air come out, so you can work with it again.

Tender:
Neither hard nor mushy. When something is tender, it is easy to stick a fork into it, but it doesn't fall apart when you do.

Puree:
Using a blender or a sieve to turn food into a smooth, thick mixture.

Toss:
Lifting and turning ingredients quickly with two forks or spoons.

Season:
Adding spices, herbs, salt or pepper to enhance the natural flavor of food.

Turn-out:
Tumbling the dough out of the bowl onto a floured board or cloth so you can knead it.

Simmer:
Cooking in liquid over low heat. It's still bubbling a little, but it's not hot enough to boil.

Glossary Activity:
If you ever find a word in a recipe you don't understand, why not look it up in the dictionary? Soon you'll become quite the expert as you continue to add words to your cooking and baking vocabulary.

The Home Baking Association has an extensive glossary of culinary terms available at HomeBaking.org.

Skewer:
Putting small pieces of food onto a bamboo or metal stick to cook or to serve. The stick is also called a skewer.

Learning About My Culture and Traditions

When a group of people shares similar traits and ways of doing things, this is known as culture. Culture is made up of many different elements including food, language, tools, customs, beliefs, religion, clothing, art, music and much more. Traditions are beliefs and customs that are passed on from generation to generation.

On the next few pages we will focus on learning about the culture and traditions in your own family.

What languages do you speak in your family?	What are some traditions in your family?
What holidays and celebrations do your family observe?	What are common foods eaten in your culture?

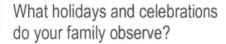

MY FAMILY

This activity provides a great opportunity to talk to your parents, grandparents, aunts and uncles about the culture and traditions in your family. Don't be afraid to ask questions because culture and traditions are something you all have in common.

Tell A Story About the Traditions In Your Family

Diwali - India

Perhaps the best example of family traditions are in relation to holiday events like Christmas, Kwanzaa, Hannukah, or the many other celebrations found around the world. Tell a story about your experiences as a family during the holiday of your choice. Do you have a particular food you like to prepare as a family? Do you travel to a different place to celebrate? Share as many details as you can remember.

Use the text box below to make notes and record your traditions.

FAMILY TRADITIONS

Your Family Culture and Traditions

Culture changes as time progresses, so the way things were when your parents and grandparents were young are probably slightly different from how things are now. Make an effort to interview your family members and find out about your family history and traditions. Use the following questions, and perhaps come up with some additional questions of your own.

Use the text box below to record answers to the following questions:

1 What kind of music did you listen to when you were young?

2 Were there any differences between education when you were young, and now?

3 What were some of the events happening in the world when you were my age?

4 Are there any resources I have now that you wish you had when you were young?

It's Time to Learn About Me!

Here is a chance for you to record some information about yourself. We'll come back to this page later in our studies to make some comparisons to the lives of children in different parts of the world. One of the really fun things about discovering world culture is you'll learn we are more alike than you think!

Answer the following questions about you!

1 What is your favorite breakfast food?

2 What do you want to be when you grow up?

3 Do you have any pets in your home?

4 What is your favorite hobby?

5 What is your neighborhood like?

6 What is your school like?

7 What kind of chores do you have in your family home?

8 What is your favorite toy?

ABOUT ME, MYSELF & I

Getting to Know World Foods

It takes a lifetime to develop an understanding of world cuisine, but learning the basics just takes a little practice. In fact, you may recognize most of the foods below. Write the letter next to the appropriate name of each dish on the page below.

PAVLOVA ___   BIBIMBAP ___

PIZZA ___   SUSHI ___

menu

A — Italy

B — The Republic of Korea

C — Japan

D — New Zealand

Being A Good Neighbor

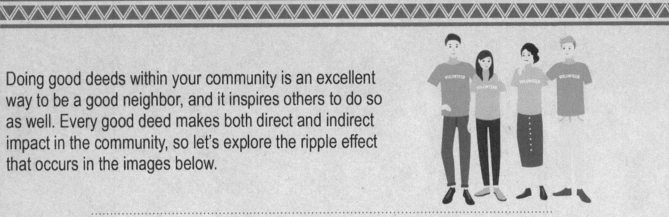

Doing good deeds within your community is an excellent way to be a good neighbor, and it inspires others to do so as well. Every good deed makes both direct and indirect impact in the community, so let's explore the ripple effect that occurs in the images below.

Identify both the direct and indirect impact each of the good deeds have in the images below.

Direct Impact: Cleaning the park makes it beautiful

Indirect Impact: More families will be inspired to visit the park and spend quality time together

Direct Impact:

Indirect Impact:

Direct Impact:

Indirect Impact:

Direct Impact:

Indirect Impact:

MY COMMUNITY

Being a good neighbor doesn't take a lot of effort. Think of the ways you can be a good neighbor in your own community.

Restavek System In Haitian Culture

Imagine if your parents couldn't afford to raise you, so you were sent to live with strangers who required you to cook and do household chores to earn your keep.

This is a way of life for many children in Haiti, a system that continues to this day. In a country plagued with poverty and natural disasters such as the 2010 earthquake, there is no end in sight for this practice. Many children in this system live in poor conditions without food and education.

Use the text box below to record answers to the following questions:

1 What are your thoughts on child slavery? How does it make you feel that some children must work to earn food and a place to sleep?

2 Education is important. How do you think a lack of education will impact the future for children in Haiti?

3 Restavek comes from the French phrase, "to stay with." How would you feel to have to stay with strangers until you became an adult?

4 Child slavery is illegal in the United States, but it still happens here and elsewhere in the world. Do a Google search to find the names of organizations who are working to end child slavery and record several names here:

CHILD SLAVERY

Inuksuk: Learning about Landmarks

An inukshuk is a manmade structure made of stones piled on top of each other. These structures were used for navigation in the far north by the Inuit and other indigenous peoples because in the blinding white snow, everything had the potential of looking the same. The structures worked as landmarks to help guide travelers and hunters to their final destinations.

A landmark can be any natural or manmade object used to help guide travelers.

Perhaps on of the most famous manmade landmarks is the Statue of Liberty. What are some other landmarks in the US?

A cairn is another manmade struction used as a landmark. From where do cairn originate?

Lighthouses are a very common landmark found all over the world. Have you visited a lighthouse before? What was the name of it, and when was it built?

LANDMARKS

What are some landmarks you recognize in your community? Is there an old barn or a tree that helps you remember how to get home? Or perhaps there is something else that helps you find your way. Think about it, you use landmarks and you didn't even realize it.

"We hold these truths to be self-evident, that all men are created equal."

American President, Thomas Jefferson

NORTH AMERICA

CANADIAN INUIT - HAWAII - CHOCTAW - HAITI - MEXICO - JAMAICA

THE DIET OF THE FAR NORTH

Most edible plants are few and far between in the cold, northern territory of the Inuit populations. Historically, most of their diet consisted of meat from hunting animals such as caribou, seal, walrus, birds, salmon and whitefish.

The short summer growing season lends itself nicely to several varieties of berries, several of which you will read as ingredients in the recipe on the next page.

Sockeye Salmon
Oncorhynchus nerka

Sockeye salmon range as far south as northern Oregon, to the Canadian Arctic in the far north. Sockeye Salmon are blue-tinged with silver while living in the Pacific Ocean, but they change to red and green when they return to spawn. They can grow to be just over two and a half feet long.

Caribou
Rangifer tarandus

Just like the seal, most parts of the caribou are used by the Inuit. The flesh is eaten, sinew is used for thread, the hide is used for clothing, and the antler are used for hunting tools. Caribou mea dries well during the summer months and can provide sustenance through the winter.

Ringed Seal
Pusa hispida

The Inuit believe the seal and the hunter have a special relationship. They believe the hunter and the seal are allowed to benefit from the relationship as the hunter provides food for his family, and the seal gets to become part of the body of the Inuit.

There is currently a population of around 2 million Ringed Seals, and Inuit hunters generally harvest around 35,000 each year. Seal is an abundant food source for the Inuit, primarily because of the many ways the Inuit use the resource. The meat can be eaten, seal hide can be used for clothing and boots, and the oil can be used for lamps.

CANADIAN INUIT

Cloudberry -
Rubus chamaemorus

Native Ice Cream (Akutaq)

This dish was traditionally made with whipped fat such as whale, seal, or caribou, then mixed with berries. However, it's very unlikely you have whale fat in your cabinets. We'll use an alternative vegetable shortening such as Crisco. While this substitution might seem unsavory to some, keep in mind one of the primary ingredients in vegetable shortening is hydrogenated palm oil, which is the same primary ingredient found in canned frosting. While I wouldn't suggest making large amounts of vegetable shortening a major component of your everyday diet, as a novelty this recipe is definitely worth trying.

Akutaq is a Yup'ik word meaning something mixed. Berries are more readily available in northern Canada and western Alaska, but cloudberries and crowberries grow in some of the coldest subarctic regions and make a perfect addition to this dish.

Huckleberry - *Vaccinium membranaceum*

19

Native Ice Cream (Akutaq)

1 Wash your hands, making sure they are very clean.

2 In a large mixing bowl, squish the vegetable shortening with your hands until the shortening is warmed by the contact with your skin. Make sure it is nice and fluffy.

3 Add the sugar and juice, and continue mixing with your hands. Make sure to try and dissolve the sugar crystals with the liquid as well as the heat from your hands. You can't mix too much!

4 Add the berries, folding them into the sugar and fat mixture without crushing them.

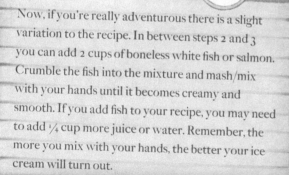

A TIP JUST FOR KIDS!

Now, if you're really adventurous there is a slight variation to the recipe. In between steps 2 and 3 you can add 2 cups of boneless white fish or salmon. Crumble the fish into the mixture and mash/mix with your hands until it becomes creamy and smooth. If you add fish to your recipe, you may need to add ¼ cup more juice or water. Remember, the more you mix with your hands, the better your ice cream will turn out.

Ideas for Continued Learning

Discover: Inuit populations live in different types of housing. Do a Google image search "Inuit Housing" and discover what form of shelter is used.

Listen: Inuit music is fascinating and very distinct. Search Youtube for "Traditional Inuit Throat Singing," and discuss with your family.

INGREDIENTS

1 cup vegetable shortening
  (Such as Crisco)
1 cup granulated sugar
¼ cup of berry juice or water
4 cups fresh berries

CANADIAN INUIT

Capital City / Ottawa, Canada	
Nation Language / Various Inuit Languages	
Canadian Inuit population / 65,000	
Currency / Canadian Dollar	

The Inuit People are spread throughout a large geographic area, encompassing parts of Canada, the United States, Greenland and Denmark. They have various governing councils in place, as well as a United Nations recognized organization called Inuit Circumpolar Council that represents their people.

A Sky Full of Stories

"There is magic in the sky," the old woman said to the little boy. They stood side by side, wrapped warm in their caribou skin hooded parkas, gazing into the night sky. The little boy enjoyed hearing his grandmother's stories about nature and the world around him. "These stars are living creatures, you know," she continued. "They once lived among us, but now are fated to wander the heavens for eternity."

Even though the boy had heard this story many times before, he listened happily to his grandmother's gentle voice. He imagined her mother, and her mother's mother, passing these stories down; telling them much in the same way.

One day, Nanuk the bear was being pursued by a pack of Inuit hunting dogs. The dogs were trained well, and they gave a good chase. Nanuk's hot breath held steady in big white puffs of air in the night sky. He ran faster than he ever had before, but he still felt the yapping of the dogs at his paws. The chase felt like it went on forever, but he was unable to shake free of them.

The hunting dogs and the bear became so engrossed in their game of life and death, neither noticed they were fast approaching the end of the world. Indeed, they soon plunged over that last cliff and fell straight into the starry abyss. To this day, when the Inuit look up into the night sky, they don't see Pleiades, in the constellation of Taurus the bull. They see Nanuk the bear and the hunting dogs in a fight to the finish.

Getting to Know the Canadian Inuit

The Inuit People are spread throughout a large geographic area, encompassing parts of Canada, the United States, Greenland and Denmark. They have various governing councils in place, as well as a United Nations recognized organization called Inuit Circumpolar Council that represents their people.

There isn't one specific flag, capital, currency, or language that represents the Inuit due to their distribution through a very large geographic area. If you'd like, you can look for videos on Youtube to listen to "Inuvialuktun," the western Canadian Inuit dialect. Also, Google the flag of the western Canadian territory "Nunavut." You will see it includes an image of the Inuit symbol, the Inuksuk.

Color this Inuit symbol, the inuksuk, a navigational landmark

Traditionally, caribou have been very important to the Inuit. Most parts of the caribou are used; the flesh is eaten, sinew is used for thread, the hide is used for clothing, and the antlers are used for hunting tools.

Hawaii

(USA)

The Hawaiian Hula is a method of storytelling through dance and intricate hand movements. It was invented by the Polynesians who first settled the islands and has become a significant part of Hawaiian culture, performed for both religious and entertainment purposes.

Hula dancers typically wear floor-length grass skirts as well as special ornamentation such as headpieces, necklaces and bracelets. Floral garlands called lei are used in ceremonies as well, with different floral and leaf patterns each carrying its own symbolism and importance.

The art form of hula requires knowledge of the many different hand motions and gestures used to tell a story. The simplest of hand movements can signify something as complex as the birth of a child or as simple as a tree swaying in the wind.

Music is an important component of Hula, with many traditional instruments used to accompany the dance. Several instruments such as the Ipu Drum and Nose Flutes are carved from hollow reeds and gourds.

Hibiscus Flower - *Hibiscus furcellatus*

Musubi Riceballs

The people of Hawaii have a complex cultural history that begins with their Polynesian beginnings. If a Hawaiian family can trace their history back many generations, they are considered native. Throughout the history of Hawaii, its natural beauty and geographic location have attracted many different groups of people to the islands.

When sugar plantations became big business in Hawaii in the 1850s, many Asian workers relocated to the islands. Today Chinese, Japanese and Filipinos make up almost 40 percent of the island population. The multi-cultural residents have integrated customs, foods and traditions from other countries into the Hawaiian way of life.

The Japanese dish Musubi has become a favorite food in Hawaii. It is prepared with either pickled plums or small wedges of luncheon meats. The small rice balls are served as a convenient snack food wrapped with a distinctive band of nori (seaweed paper).

The tradition of May Day in Hawaii is a little different. Hawaiians give the gift of a lei accompanied by a kiss for good luck on May 1st each year.

How to Make Your Own Lei

Step 1 - Cut an appropriate length of string to hang like a necklace (16-20 inches depending on your size). Make a knot at one end of the string.

Step 2 - Create and cut 10-15 flowers from brightly colored paper. Do the same with 10-15 leaves on green paper, making sure the leaves are just a bit larger than the flowers.

Step 3 - Using a hole punch, create a small hole in the exact center of each piece.

Step 4 - Count how many flowers and leaves you have in total. Cut that many 1½-inch long pieces of drinking straws.

Step 5 - String all of your pieces on the string, creating a leaf, flower, straw pattern. Make a knot after the last piece, then tie both ends of the string together to form your very own lei.

Musubi Riceballs

1 Soak the rice for one hour, then prepare as directed on packaging.

2 Cut two sheets of nori into nine strips about ¾-inch wide.

3 Remove the pits from the umeboshi and pat dry with a paper towel.

4 Wet your hands then mold a handful of rice into a 2-inch ball.

5 Sprinkle with sesame seeds.

6 Press a piece of umeboshi into the center

7 Place a band of nori around the outer edge of the ball.

Continue assembling the Musubi until you've exhausted your supplies. You may sprinkle each rice ball with sesame seeds or aonori if desired.

A TIP JUST FOR KIDS

"I think you should try umeboshi because it is something new and different. If you really don't like it, try pressing dried apricot or a fresh grape in the center instead."

Ideas for Continued Learning

Listen: Research "Hawaiian Mele and Chants" on Youtube to listen to traditional Hawaiian music.

Taste: Hawaii is known for natural resources such as sugarcane, pineapple and macadamia nuts. Taste these delicious treats.

INGREDIENTS

3 cups sticky rice (glutinous rice or sweet rice)

1¼ cups water

4 sheets nori (seaweed paper)

4 to 5 umeboshi (pickled plums)

2 teaspoons toasted sesame seeds

Salt (to taste)

OPTIONAL INGREDIENTS

Aonori (crushed green seaweed)

Sesame seeds

HAWAII

Capital City / Honolulu	
Nation Language / English, Hawaiian	
Population / 1,392,313	
Currency / Dollar	

United States of America *is comprised of fifty states, with Hawaii being the most recent addition on August 21, 1959. The state of Hawaii is actually a group of more than eight islands with the city of Honolulu as their capital.*

The Hawaiian Naupaka Legend

There once was a Hawaiian maiden who lived high on the mountain. Every day she traveled down the slopes to the ocean shore where she bathed and played in the sun. One day a vibrant green honu (Hawaiian Green Sea Turtle, *Chelonia mydas*) saw the girl and became enchanted by her beauty. But the turtle was actually a kupua, a shape-shifting trickster god who could take on any appearance he liked.

Overwhelmed by his love for the girl, the kupua turned himself into a handsome young man and bodysurfed to the shore. The young man professed his love for the girl and each day when she came to the water's edge they would splash and play until sunset. The girl then returned to the mountain each night.

Disheartened by her departure every evening, the young man proposed to the girl one afternoon. Together they found a village elder and asked him to perform the marriage ceremony. But the elder realized the young man was actually a shape-shifter kupua, and consequently a marriage between the two was forbidden.

Frustrated, the kupua found a beautiful white flower blossoming on a nearby tree. He gave half of one of the blossoms to the girl and left the other half on the tree. With tears in his eyes, he told the girl if she wished to see him again, she would bring her flower to this tree and reunite it with its other half. He would then return from the ocean and they would be together again.

Green Sea Turtle - *Chelonia mydas*

Getting to Know Hawaii

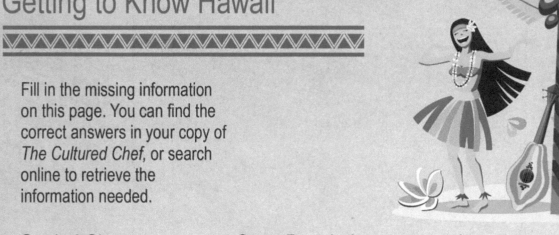

Fill in the missing information on this page. You can find the correct answers in your copy of *The Cultured Chef*, or search online to retrieve the information needed.

Capital City:

State Population:

Languages:

Google Hawaii's flag and use as reference to color the drawing below.

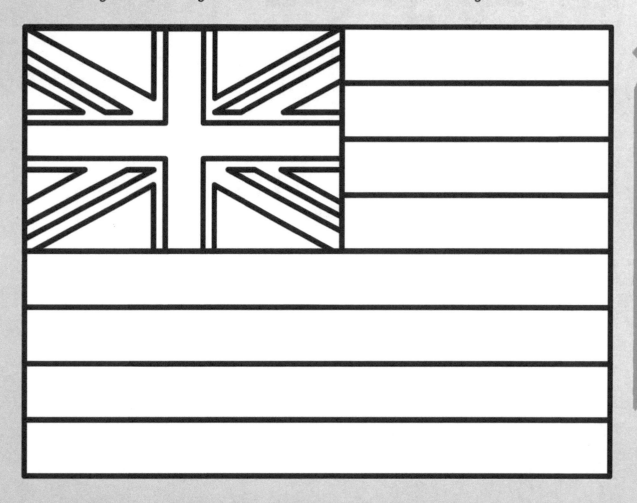

HAWAII

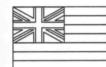

The Hawaiian Islands

Produced by a volcanic hotspot rising
from the depths of the Pacific Ocean,
the Hawaiian Islands are an archipelago
that formed nearly 75 million years ago.
While 8 of the islands are well-known by
tourists, there are actually 137 islands that
make up the chain of islands.

THE NATIVE AMERICAN DIET

The Three Sisters

Indigenous populations throughout the Americas have been planting these three main agricultural groups for a very long time. Known as The Three Sisters, the crops are comprised of winter squash, corn, and climbing beans. Grouping these plants together in a designated growing area is known as companion planting.

Squash, corn and beans grow together harmoniously when planting is scheduled such that each of the plants can benefit from the others. Several corn seeds are first planted in the center of a flattened mound. When the corn reaches 6 inches tall, beans and squash are planted alternately in a circle surrounding the small plants. Eventually, the beans will grow up the corn stalks and the leafy mounds of the squash will cool the ground, prevent weeds from overtaking the crops, and minimize pests due to the prickly hairs on the vines.

Almost every Native American group planted some variation of the Three Sisters.

1. Winter Squash is an annual fruit that hardens with a thick outer skin that allows growers to store the fruit for many months.

2. Corn was first domesticated over 8,000 years ago by indigenous peoples in southern Mexico.

3. Beans are grown on every continent except Antarctica. Native American populations planted climbing varieties that grew up in to corn stalks.

CHOCTAW NATIVE AMERICAN (USA)

Choctaw Horse
- *Equus caballus*

Maize (or Corn) - *Zea mays*

Banaha Bread

The Choctaw are a Native American people who originated from the Southeastern United States in the area now known as Florida, Alabama, Mississippi and Louisiana. It is believed their name comes from the phrase, Hacha hatak, which means River People.

Food is a very important part of any Choctaw gathering, with dishes like this being prepared at family gatherings such as weddings and funerals. The ingredients are very inexpensive, and can be grown in the family garden.

Banaha Bread

1 Boil the corn husks for about 10 minutes to soften.

2 Mix the dry ingredients, then add water and continue mixing until the mixture is stiff enough to handle easily. You can use your hands if you like.

3 Form small oval-shaped balls the size of a tennis ball and place in the center of a corn husk. Wrap the dough with the husks and tie securely so it forms a little package.

4 Drop the wrapped dough into a deep pot of boiling water. Cover and cook for 40 minutes.

A TIP JUST FOR KIDS!

Be careful when removing the Banaha Bread from the water as it is very hot. Wait several minutes for the bread to cool down, then unwrap. You can be creative in how you'd like to eat the bread. Serve with beans, gravy, or whatever side dish interests you.

INGREDIENTS

2 cups cornmeal

1 1/2 cups hot water

1 teaspoon baking soda

1 teaspoon salt

A handful of corn husks

Durable string or twine

Ideas for Continued Learning

Learn: Research "Pushmataha," one of the most famous Choctaw chiefs. When did he live and what is he known for?

Draw: Choctaw design used in beadwork and weaving is beautiful. Search for examples of "Choctaw patterns" online and try drawing them on your own.

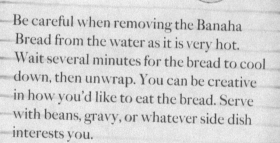

CHOCTAW

Capital City / Washington, DC

Nation Language / English, Choctaw

Choctaw Population / 223,000

Currency / Dollar

Perhaps you've heard of the game called stickball? The game was invented by the Choctaw people, and it is thought to be one of the oldest team sports in North America. Historically it was played for entertainment and as a way to settle disputes.

All the Poisonous Creatures

For many years there was certain trouble in the shallow coastal waters. The Choctaw people used these waters to bathe and swim, but a mysterious vine grew rapidly, choking the shallow water and spreading its poison. The vine was very apologetic for this offense, often saying, "I'm sorry to cause you problems." The brave men tried to cut the vine, but doing so only made its poison become even more dangerous.

One day, the vine called a meeting with the other creatures of the bayou. Spiders, bees, snakes, fire ants and many other creatures came to hear what she had to say. "I have loved the Choctaw people for many years, but my poison is growing ever more dangerous and something must be done." The creatures listened intently. "I have decided to give away my poison. Each of you can take a small amount for yourselves, and together we can make the water safe again."

The creatures of the bayou spoke amongst themselves, considering the vine's suggestion. The bee was the first to agree with the plan. "My hive is often disturbed by larger creatures. If I had a small amount of poison, I could use it to strike fear in the hearts of those who might harm my home." One by one, each of the creatures agreed a little bit of poison was much better than having too much. The creatures agreed to take the vine's poison, and the water was made safe for the people once more.

Western Honey Bee -
Apis mellifera

Getting to Know the Choctaw

Fill in the missing information on this page. You can find the correct answers in your copy of *The Cultured Chef,* or search online to retrieve the information needed.

Language:

Tribal Population:

Google the Choctaw flag and use as reference to color the drawing below.

CHOCTAW

These days most Choctaw citizens live in modern houses and dress in modern clothing. But the Choctaw people work to celebrate their unique culture by remembering their distinct laguages, historical games, native dances and ceremonies.

HAITI

Vodou: A Way of Life In Haiti

Brought to Haiti by slaves who arrived more than three hundred years ago, Vodou means "spirit" in several African languages. Believers recognize a distant creator named Bondye who is detached and unknowable and is represented by many spirits called Loa. Haitians perform rituals in the form of songs, dances and by creating altars in an effort to connect with and please these spirits.

Each of the spirits has his or her own unique personality, so believers of Vodou can choose which Loa they feel most connected to. During ceremonies the Loa are given food and drink in the hope they will offer special advice or words of wisdom.

Papa Guaédé

An example of one of the many Loa celebrated in Vodou is Papa Guédé, believed to be the skeleton of the first man who ever died. His primary role is to help people transition from life to death, but he's also regarded as a protector of children. If a child is sick, people will pray to Papa Guédé to spare the child's life.

Haitian Freedom Soup

For over one hundred years, the French controlled Haiti, taking advantage of the many natural resources and growing conditions the land had to offer. In order to farm massive amounts of sugar, coffee, cotton and indigo on their plantations, the French imported nearly one million slaves from Africa. Today a major percentage of Haiti's population traces their ancestry to the African slaves.

The French plantation owners treated the slaves terribly, offering them only the minimum of what they needed to survive. While the slaves dined on a thin bread soup, the plantation owners enjoyed a rich and hearty pumpkin soup. In fact, the slaves were forbidden to eat the soup because it was considered too fancy for the simple people.

After more than one hundred years, the people of Haiti were fed up with the French. They began fighting back in 1791 and after a long battle won their independence! What was one of the first things they did following their victory? They celebrated by eating pumpkin soup! To this day, pumpkin soup is served in millions of homes every year on January 1 as a reminder of Haitian independence.

Haitian Freedom Soup

 1 In a large pot, add the pumpkin and water, stirring until it reaches an even consistency.

 2 Press cloves halfway into the flesh of the pepper, then add to pumpkin mixture.

 3 Add carrots, cabbage, nutmeg, lime juice and zest, salt and pepper. Cover and bring to a boil.

 4 Reduce heat to medium-low and simmer for 10 minutes. Stir in macaroni, parsley and coconut milk, cover again and simmer gently until pasta is tender and soup is thickened, about 10 minutes more. Add more water to thin the soup if you find it too thick.

 5 Be creative with your presentation. Serve with a dollop of sour cream and a sprinkle of crushed pistachios or whatever else you like.

A TIP JUST FOR KIDS

"I love making designs with pumpkin seeds on top of this soup. You can buy different flavors of roasted pumpkin seeds at the store, or you can look up instructions online on how to make your own at home."

Ideas for Continued Learning

Listen: Search for "Haitian Folktales for Children" online to listen to traditional stories from Haiti.

Taste: February 8 th is National Kite Flying Day. Research this festivity online, and make a kite of your own.

INGREDIENTS

2 pounds fresh pumpkin
(2 cups mashed)
10 cups water, plus more if needed
1 13.5-ounce can of unsweetened coconut milk
1 jalapeño or serrano pepper
10 whole cloves
4 carrots, peeled and sliced
1/2 small head green cabbage, cored and chopped
1/2 teaspoon ground nutmeg
1 tablespoon curry powder
medium lime (zest and juice)
1/4 pound macaroni
1/4 cup chopped parsley
Salt and pepper to taste

HAITI

Capital City / Port-au- Prince

Nation Language / French

Population / 9,719,932

Currency / Gourde

Haiti occupies a smaller portion of the island of Hispaniola, which it shares with the Spanish-speaking country the Dominican Republic. The name of the country is derived from the native Taíno word *Ayiti*, meaning "land of high mountains."

Uncle Bouki and Ti Malice: A Haitian Folktale

One fine morning, Uncle Bouki was walking down the lane when his stomach began kicking and dancing; he was very hungry! While he rushed home to prepare a meal for himself, he saw a toothless old woman eating alongside the road.

"Mmmm, that looks delicious," Uncle Bouki said. "What are you eating?" Distracted by the nosey Uncle Bouki, the old woman bit her lip and screamed out, "Ay-yai!"

With no time to lose, Uncle Bouki raced to the market in search of some delicious ay-yai for himself. The poor man was very hungry indeed! But when he arrived at the market and began asking questions, the vendors only laughed at him because ay-yai didn't exist at all!

"I'm so hungry, I can't think of anything else," Uncle Bouki said to Ti Malice when he returned home. "Do you have any ay-yai?"

Ti Malice wanted to teach silly Uncle Bouki a lesson, so he gathered a number of items and placed them in a bag. "Here's your ay-yai; it's the best I have."

Uncle Bouki pulled out an orange from the bag and said, "No, this isn't what I'm looking for." Next, he pulled out a pineapple and just shook his head. "No, not this one either." Finally, he reached into the bag and pulled out a piece of cactus.

"Ay-yai, ay-yai!" screamed Uncle Bouki as the prickly cactus spines poked into his skin. "What did you do that for?" he asked. Ti Malice couldn't control his laughter and answered, "You asked for some Ay-yai, and that's just what you got!"

Getting to Know Haiti

Fill in the missing information on this page. You can find the correct answers in your copy of *The Cultured Chef*, or search online to retrieve the information needed.

Capital City:

Country Population:

Languages:

Google the flag for Haiti and use as reference to color the drawing below.

Haiti: The National Flower Hibiscus

Hibiscus is a tropical flower that grows in warm and sunny climates around the world. It has been adpoted as the national flower of Haiti

MEXICO

DAY OF THE DEAD

If you were to imagine Halloween and Memorial Day combined, how do you think the celebration would go? Chances are it would look a lot like Dia de Los Muertos (Day of the Dead). The Mexican holiday honors those who have died with a national fiesta complete with food, music, flowers and art.

Sagrado Corazón de Jesús

Catrina

Day of the Dead wouldn't be complete without the Catrina, created by artist Jose Guadalupe Posada in the early 1900s. She is a fancy skeleton lady dressed in expensive dresses with big scarves and floppy hats. She was designed to remind the people that everyone faces death similarly, whether they are rich or poor.

Frida

Catrina in Mexican folk art may take many forms. For example, the Catrina represented on the left side of this page is in the style of artist Frida Kahlo. Kahlo began painting after a terrible bus accident left her severely injured. During her life, she spent countless hours confined to her bed where she painted self-portraits to pass the time. Today, some of those self-portraits have gone on to sell for more than a million dollars.

Monarch Butterfly - *Danaus plexippus*

SUGAR SKULLS
Mexican Sugar Skulls - Calaveras de Azúcar
EACH SKULL REPRESENTS A DEPARTED SOUL, WITH HIS OR HER NAME WRITTEN ON THE FOREHEAD.

Day of the Dead Bread
(Pan de Muerte)

Every year on the evening of November 1, cemeteries all over Mexico are filled to the brim with families celebrating their loved ones who have passed away. Complete with music and food, the celebration feels more like a birthday party than a funeral. It often lasts until the early morning hours with plenty to eat and drink. Bread and Day of the Dead go hand-in-hand.

Bakeries on every street corner sell the sweet, round bread in the days leading up to November 1. Loaves are available in many different sizes and often have small decorations baked into them in the shape of tear drops, hearts, flowers and bones. These rolls are placed with the flowers and decorations until they are eaten in the morning when families prepare to return home.

Some Like It Hot:
If there is one vegetable that best represents Mexican cuisine, it is the chili pepper. What kind of peppers do you like? Research the different varieties of peppers available, and, if you can take the heat, try one or two the next time you're at the market.

Bread of the Dead

1 In a medium saucepan, heat the milk and butter together until the butter melts completely. Remove the mixture from the heat and add 1/4 cup warm water (it should be around 110 degrees Fahrenheit).

2 In a large bowl, combine the all-purpose flour, yeast, salt, anise seed and sugar. Beat in the warm milk mixture, then add eggs and orange zest and beat until well combined. Stir in ½ cup of flour, then continue adding more flour until the dough is soft.

3 Turn the dough out onto a lightly floured surface and knead until smooth and elastic.

4 Place the dough in a lightly greased bowl, cover with plastic wrap and let rise in a warm place until doubled in size. This will take about one to two hours. Punch the dough down and shape it into a large round loaf. Place dough onto a baking sheet, loosely cover with plastic wrap and let rise in a warm place for about one hour or until nearly doubled in size.

5 Bake in a preheated 350 degree Fahrenheit oven for about 35 to 45 minutes. Remove from the oven, let cool slightly then brush with glaze.

6 To make the glaze: In a small saucepan combine sugar, orange juice and orange zest. Bring to a boil over medium heat and boil for two minutes. Brush over the top of bread while still warm. Sprinkle glazed bread with white sugar.

A TIP JUST FOR KIDS!

"I like using small pieces of leftover dough to make designs on top of my loaves before they go in the oven. You can make bones, rays of a sun or anything else you can imagine!"

Ideas for Continued Learning

Watch: Search "Monarch Butterfly Migration" on Youtube. Learn where these butterflies spend their winters.

Experience: Cartonería, or Paper Mache, is a popular craft in Mexico. Find instructions and create some art of your own.

INGREDIENTS

1/4 cup unsalted butter

1/4 cup milk

1/4 cup warm water

3 cups all-purpose flour

1 1/4 teaspoons active dry yeast

1/2 teaspoon salt

2 teaspoons anise seed

1/4 cup sugar

2 large eggs, beaten

2 teaspoon orange zest

INGREDIENTS - GLAZE

1/4 cup sugar

1/4 cup orange juice

1 tablespoon orange zest

MEXICO

Capital City / Mexico City

Nation Language / Spanish

Population / 117,409,830

Currency / Peso

Mexico is the site of several ancient civilizations including the Olmec, Toltec, Zapotec, Mayan and Aztec peoples. Each civilization has made an impact on the culture and traditions of the country.

Marigold - Tagetes erecta

What is an Altar?

Altars (Ofrenda) offer a way for people to remember their loved ones who have passed away. Although most altars are in private homes, many are on display publicly in the community as well.

An altar represents the four elements of nature: Earth, Wind, Water and Fire. Here's a brief overview of each of those elements.

Earth - is represented by agricultural elements like fruit or vegetables. The aroma of the food gives the dead an opportunity to replenish their energy after their long journey home.

Wind - is represented by objects that flutter in the breeze like colorful paper cutouts called papel picado or bundles of wheat or corn.

Water - is always available for the departed in either a pitcher with glasses or a bottle. Water also signifies purity and renewal.

Fire - is represented in altars by candles of all shapes and sizes. The flames help to attract spirits who might have lost their way.

The Mexican Marigold

Marigold flowers are known in Mexico as Cempasúchil and are often referred to as the Flower of the Dead. They are used extensively in altars because it is believed their strong odor and bright color help guide the spirits home.

Do It Yourself: Plant your own marigold flowers at home this spring! Whether you are looking for flowers big or small, marigolds provide blooms all summer long.

Getting to Know Mexico

Fill in the missing information on this page. You can find the correct answers in your copy of *The Cultured Chef,* or search online to retrieve the information needed.

Capital City:

Country Population:

Language:

Google Mexico's flag and use as reference to color the drawing below.

MEXICO

El Castillo

Chichén Itzá

Mexico had a long and complex history before the arrival of the Europeans that eventually settled there. There are remnents of the ancient civilizations throughout the country, with ruins from the Maya, Toltec, Zapotec and Mixtec people still viewable today.

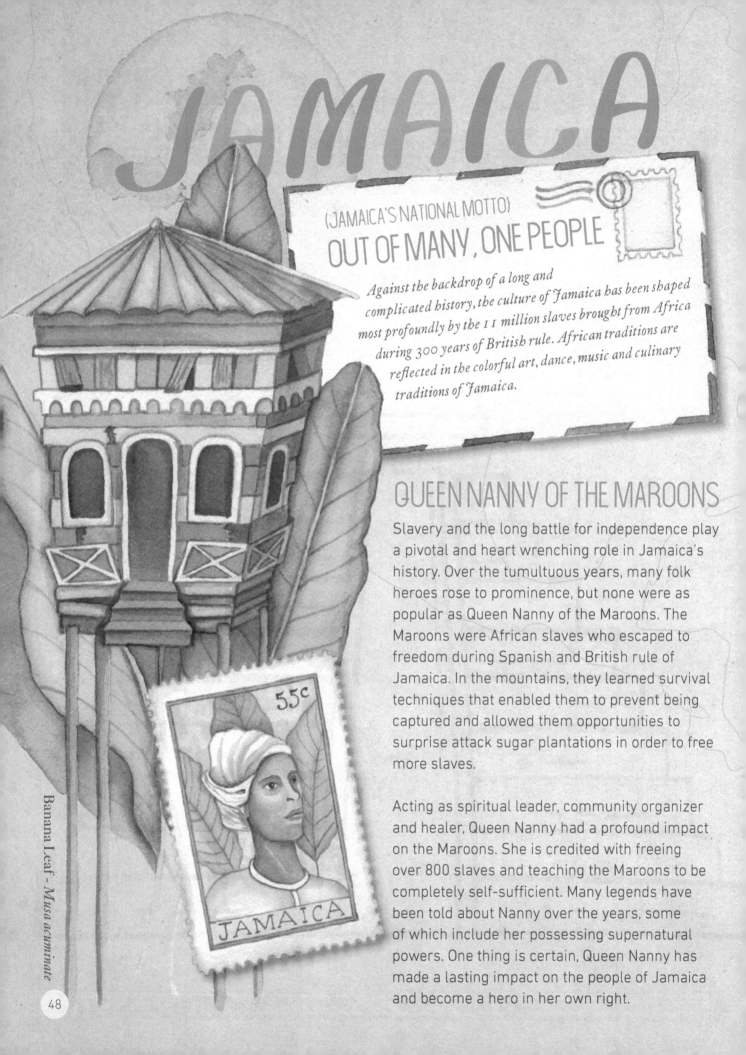

JAMAICA

JAMAICA

(JAMAICA'S NATIONAL MOTTO)

OUT OF MANY, ONE PEOPLE

Against the backdrop of a long and complicated history, the culture of Jamaica has been shaped most profoundly by the 11 million slaves brought from Africa during 300 years of British rule. African traditions are reflected in the colorful art, dance, music and culinary traditions of Jamaica.

QUEEN NANNY OF THE MAROONS

Slavery and the long battle for independence play a pivotal and heart wrenching role in Jamaica's history. Over the tumultuous years, many folk heroes rose to prominence, but none were as popular as Queen Nanny of the Maroons. The Maroons were African slaves who escaped to freedom during Spanish and British rule of Jamaica. In the mountains, they learned survival techniques that enabled them to prevent being captured and allowed them opportunities to surprise attack sugar plantations in order to free more slaves.

Acting as spiritual leader, community organizer and healer, Queen Nanny had a profound impact on the Maroons. She is credited with freeing over 800 slaves and teaching the Maroons to be completely self-sufficient. Many legends have been told about Nanny over the years, some of which include her possessing supernatural powers. One thing is certain, Queen Nanny has made a lasting impact on the people of Jamaica and become a hero in her own right.

55¢

JAMAICA

Banana Leaf - Musa acuminate

SHRIMP JERK SKEWERS

We don't often hear the word "jerk" associated with food in the United States, but in Jamaica it has been for many years. Jerk is a style of cooking in which meat is either rubbed or marinated in a blend of spices before cooking. And we're not talking about a couple spices here — traditional jerk seasoning recipes include 15-20 ingredients for a mouth-wateringly complex combination of flavors!

We're using shrimp in this recipe because the Jamaicans have a special place in their hearts for this shellfish. In a region called the Middle Quarters, Jamaican street food vendors line the streets selling plastic bags of bright red shrimp to locals and tourists alike. Wearing white aprons and cooking over hissing grills and bubbling pots, the cooks call out and wave their bags of shrimp to passing cars and trucks all day long.

Shrimp - *Pandalus borealis*

Shrimp - *Pandalus borealis*: are small free-swimming crustaceans (the same family as crabs and lobsters) that are harvested worldwide as a food source.

The story of sugar cane and Jamaica go hand in hand. For over 150 years, millions of African slaves were transported to Jamaica to aid in the cultivation of sugar cane. The plant represents millions of dollars earned for farmers and continues to be an important crop for Jamaica today.

WELCOME TO MIDDLE QUARTERS SHRIMP COUNTRY

SHRIMP JERK SKEWERS

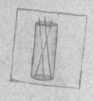

1. Prepare bamboo skewers by soaking them in water for 20 minutes.

2. In a large mixing bowl, whisk together the jerk seasoning, 1/3 cup olive oil and ginger.

3. Add shrimp and pineapple to the mixture and evenly coat. Cover and let marinate for 15 minutes.

4. Skewer the shrimp and pineapple alternately and place them on a baking sheet lined with aluminum foil. Squeeze fresh lime juice over the kebabs and season with a dash of salt and pepper. Preheat broiler.

5. Cook until the pineapple is tender and the shrimp are opaque, turning the skewers once during the process (about 4-5 minutes per side).

Instructions for making Jerk Seasoning:

Combine the following:

- 1 tablespoon salt
- 1 teaspoon ground allspice
- 2 teaspoons brown sugar
- 1 teaspoon garlic powder
- 1 teaspoon onion powder
- ½ teaspoon paprika
- ½ teaspoon ground nutmeg
- ½ teaspoon black pepper
- ½ teaspoon ground ginger
- ¼ teaspoon ground cinnamon
- ¼ teaspoon ground cloves
- ¼ teaspoon dried thyme
- ¼ teaspoon red pepper flakes

When ready to prepare your dish, use dry or mix to desired consistency using olive oil.

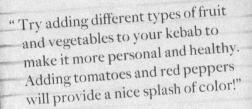

A TIP JUST FOR KIDS!

" Try adding different types of fruit and vegetables to your kebab to make it more personal and healthy. Adding tomatoes and red peppers will provide a nice splash of color!"

Ideas for Continued Learning

Watch: Search "Miss Lou Anancy" on Youtube. Miss Lou is an important Jamaican storyteller.

Experience: Allspice (or pimento) is a popular ingredient found in Jamaican food. Taste it, smell it, and learn how it is used.

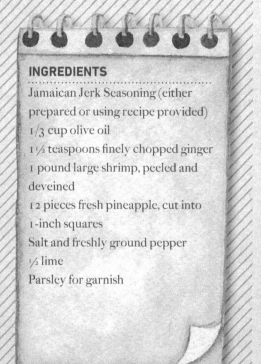

INGREDIENTS

Jamaican Jerk Seasoning (either prepared or using recipe provided)

1/3 cup olive oil

1½ teaspoons finely chopped ginger

1 pound large shrimp, peeled and deveined

12 pieces fresh pineapple, cut into 1-inch squares

Salt and freshly ground pepper

½ lime

Parsley for garnish

JAMAICA

Capital City / Kingston	
Nation Language / English	
Population / 2,88,187	
Currency / Jamaican Dollar	

Jamaica *is "the fairest island that eyes have beheld,"* Christopher Columbus exclaimed when he became the first European to visit the island in 1494. The native population thought so as well when they named their island Xaymaca, meaning "the land of wood and water."

Queen Conch - *Lobatus gigas*

ANANCY:
THE JAMAICAN SPIDER MAN

Always very clever, Anancy the spider man decided to collect all of the wisdom of the world to keep it safe. He looked for wisdom in all the places he'd left it, and when he was happy with what he'd found, he safely tucked it into a big cauldron with a tight lid. At first, he was pleased with his work, but soon Anancy began to have doubts. "What if someone finds the cauldron and keeps all the wisdom for himself?" he thought. So the crafty spider began looking for a new place to hide all the wisdom of the world.

Finding himself in front of a very large tamarind tree, Anancy decided he'd found the perfect hiding spot. He began pushing his heavy load up the tree but found the weight of the cauldron was too great. Happening upon this scene, Anancy's son cried out, "Father, what are you doing? If you want to carry the cauldron up the tree, you should tie it behind you. That way you can grip the tree!"

Frustrated he didn't come up with the idea himself, Anancy threw his legs up in disgrace accidentally letting the cauldron crash to the ground. With that, all the wisdom of the world tumbled into a nearby stream where it was eventually carried to the four corners of the earth. Because of Anancy's carelessness, now there is a little bit of wisdom for everybody!

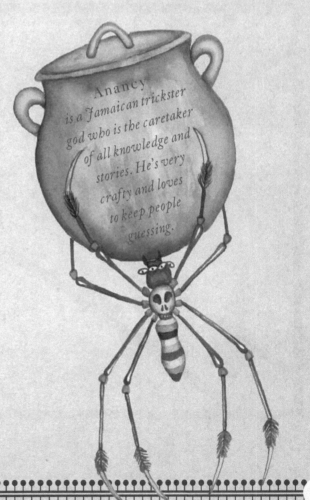

Anancy is a Jamaican trickster god who is the caretaker of all knowledge and stories. He's very crafty and loves to keep people guessing.

Getting to Know Jamaica

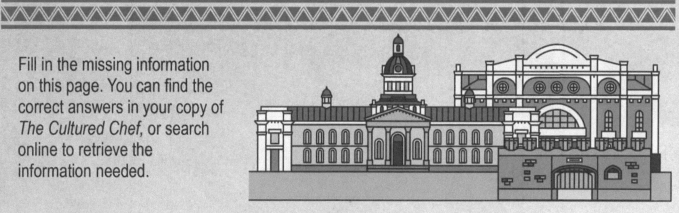

Fill in the missing information on this page. You can find the correct answers in your copy of *The Cultured Chef*, or search online to retrieve the information needed.

Capital City:

Country Population:

Language:

Google Jamaica's flag and use as reference to color the drawing below.

JAMAICA

Color the World!

Jamaica - "Doctor Bird"

The beautiful "Doctor Bird" or Swallow-Tail Hummingbird is one of the most popular symbols of Jamaica. The bird is native to Jamaica, and has not been found living elsewhere.

The Flora and Fauna of North America

North America is the third largest continent in size and the fourth largest when population is taken into consideration. There are 23 countries residing in North America, with the bulk of the continent positioned in the Northern Hemisphere and the Western Hemisphere. See what plants and animals you recognize in this region.

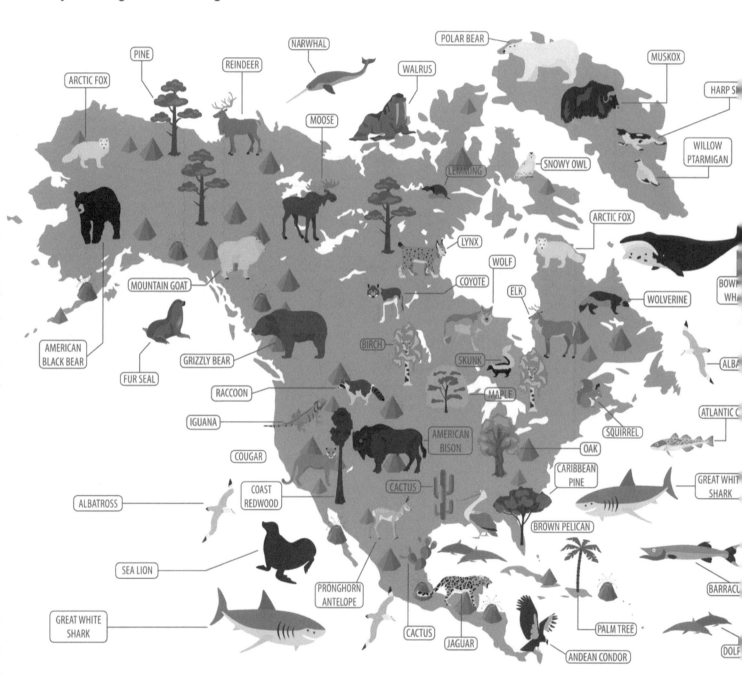

Animals
of North America

There is a lot to consider when learning about animals of the world. Different animals are suited to different climates, and have particular tastes when it comes to the food they need to survive. A penguin won't feel very much at home on the beach in Miami, Florida, would it?

Select an animal from the previous page about North America and write a short report below. Where does the animal live? What does the animal like to eat? Are there any other facts about this animal you find interesting?

Use the space below to write down interesting facts about the animal you have chosen.

NORTH AMERICA

"Shadows cannot see themselves in the mirror of the sun."

First Lady of Argentina, Eva Perón

SOUTH AMERICA

ECUADOR - ARGENTINA - BRAZIL - COLOMBIA

ECUADOR

Charles Darwin & the Voyage of the Beagle

In September 1835, a 22-year-old British naturalist named Charles Darwin spent five weeks in the Galápagos charting the geology of the islands. He didn't realize it at the time, but the observations he made and the specimens he collected during those weeks would change science forever. He eventually became one of the most famous naturalists in the world due in part to his theories on natural selection introduced in his book "On the Origin of the Species", published in 1859.

Galápagos Tortoise - Chelonoidis nis

The Magnificent Galápagos Islands

The Galápagos Islands are located in the Pacific Ocean six hundred miles west of Ecuador. Constant undersea volcanic activity created this group of islands (archipelago) comprised of 14 large islands and many smaller ones. Throughout the history of the region, every time a volcano erupted, mounds of lava hardened and grew higher and higher until an island was formed. Some of the islands are still growing!

Magnificent Frigatebird - Fregata magnificens

Sally Lightfoot Crab - Grapsus grapsus

Poison Dart Frog - Ranitomeya amazonica

Lava Lizard - Microlophus albemarlensis

The Galápagos Islands experience pleasant weather, plenty of food and nutrients, and limited exposure to predators and humans. These special circumstances have allowed the diverse plant and animal species in the region to flourish for thousands of years. In fact, a number of these species are not found anywhere else in the world.

58

Guineafowl Pufferfish - *Arothron meleagris*

Shrimp Ceviche with Tomato Sauce
(Ceviche de Langostinos)

Seafood is by far the most popular food along the Ecuadorian coast, with shrimp, crab and clams encompassing a significant part of the everyday diet. Ceviche is a traditional dish enjoyed by locals and tourists alike. It includes a selection of healthy and delicious ingredients that are widely available and relatively inexpensive.

There is a lot of debate about where ceviche originates. Some people believe the dish comes from Perú originally, while others say Polynesians invented the tasty treat. Wherever ceviche comes from, everyone agrees it is delicious and easy to prepare.

The shrimp in ceviche isn't the only seafood Ecuadorians enjoy; the region is home to over 800 species of fish! In western Ecuador, the nutrient-rich waters that lead into the Amazon are full of fish and amphibians that can't be found anywhere else in the world. The fish of Ecuador are a wonder to behold.

Blue Footed Booby
"The bird is well known for its big blue feet, which it uses to attract females during mating season. The bigger and brighter the booby's feet are, the more attractive he appears to the female he is wooing."

Blue Footed Booby - *Sula nebouxii*

Longnose Hawkfish - *Oxycirrhites typus*

Shrimp Ceviche with Tomato Sauce

 **1** Dice the onion into the thinnest and smallest possible pieces.

 2 Place the onion pieces in a bowl of cold, salted water and soak for 20 minutes.

 3 Rinse shrimp with cold water and set aside.

 4 Drain onions and rinse with cold water. Combine onions and corn with the shrimp.

 **5** In a small bowl, whisk together lime juice, orange juice, ketchup, sugar and vinegar. Toss with shrimp, corn, cilantro and onions. Allow the seafood to "cook" in the acidic liquid until it is opaque. Season to taste with salt and pepper.

A TIP JUST FOR KIDS!

"Have you ever tried serving ceviche in a hollowed out avocado? It's delicious! Remove the pit from an avocado as well as a little bit of the meat. Replace that area with a nice scoop of ceviche."

Ideas for Continued Learning

Learn: There is little fluctuation in seasons near the equator, Google "Equatorial seasons and climate" and learn about this unique climate.

Make: Ecuadorian arts and crafts use bright colors and bold patterns. Google "Ecuadorian Masks" and paint your own face mask using a paper plate.

INGREDIENTS

2-3 cups of bay shrimp

½ medium red onion, minced

Juice of 1 regular lime

¼ cup of fresh squeezed
 orange juice

½ cup ketchup

1 tablespoon white vinegar

1 tablespoon white sugar

1 cup of canned corn, drained

½ cup of packed cilantro leaves

Juvenile King Angelfish
- Holacanthus passer

ECUADOR

Capital City / Quito	
Nation Language / Spanish	
Population / 15,223,680	
Currency / Dollar	

Ecuador is the Spanish word for equator; a name aptly given to the country situated directly in on The Equator, an imaginary line that divides the Northern and Southern hemispheres, essentially dividing the earth in half.

The Children of the Sun: The Incan Empire

Many years ago a small tribe of natives built a city named Cuzco in what is now known as Peru. The Incas were a peaceful tribe who worshipped the sun god Inti and believed their leader was the child of the sun.

In 1438 their simple way of life was threatened when a neighboring tribe called the Chancay unsuccessfully tried to conquer them. Little did the Incas know that this battle would be the impetus to them becoming a great and mighty empire!

Over the next 100 years, the Incas conquered neighboring tribes until their empire stretched over an area 2,500 miles long and 500 miles wide. Their kingdom included much of what is now known as Ecuador, and their little tribe swelled to include more than 12 million people.

As mighty as the Incas were, the arrival of Spanish invaders and a massive epidemic of smallpox devastated them. In just a few short years, between 60 to 90 percent of the Incan population was destroyed.

SUN GOD - INTI

Getting to Know Ecuador

Fill in the missing information on this page. You can find the correct answers in your copy of *The Cultured Chef,* or search online to retrieve the information needed.

Capital City:

Country Population:

Language:

Google Ecuador's flag and use as reference to color the drawing below.

ECUADOR

Ecuador - The Galapagos Islands

The Galapagos Tortoises average a lifespan of over 100 years. In fact, the oldest on record lived to be 152! They are also very large, with some exceeding 5 feet in length and weighing in at 550 pounds.

MUSICAL INSTRUMENTS OF THE WORLD

Can you even imagine a world without music? Consider all of the ways music has shaped your life. Do you remember your mother and father singing lullabies to you as a young child? Did you ever make up little songs to help you better learn lessons in school? Did you pass the time on long car rides with music? These are just some of the simple, everyday examples of how music impacts our lives.

Sompoton: From Northeastern Borneo, this gourd and pipe instrument is still played by the Kadasan and Dusun people. The instrument can be played in any number of orientations and can range anywhere from 6 inches to 3 feet in length. Do you think you can make your own homemade version of this instrument? Each pipe is fitted with a bamboo reed then placed in exact formation to create two rows of four pipes each, producing a complex and beautiful sound.

Marimba: Configured much in the same way as a xylophone, the marimba is a large instrument with hollowed out wooden bars that produce various tones when struck with mallets. While many cultures now include the marimba as part of their traditional music, the instrument as we know it today originates from the Garifuna people of Guatemala.

Bagpipes: The bagpipes have become such an important part of Scottish culture, it is impossible to think of the country without considering this unique instrument. But, did you know that the bagpipes didn't originate in Scotland? It is believed goat and sheep herdsmen in Samaria first made music out of animal skin and reed pipes. In fact, there are mentions of instruments resembling the bagpipes in the Old Testament of the Bible.

Accordian: A traditional instrument of folk music, the accordion has become a worldwide phenomenon that has even found its way into mainstream pop music. For thousands of years, there have been many instruments manufactured using the basic principles of the accordion, but it is believed the instrument we recognize today was created by the German instrument maker Christian Friedrich Ludwig Buschmann in 1822.

Chau Gong: Dating back to the Chinese Han Dynasty around 200 BC, the chau gong has been used for centuries to announce the presence of important officials or political figures. Typically suspended from a sturdy frame and ranging from 7 to 80 inches in diameter, the gong is struck with a mallet to produce a rich tone. These ancient musical instruments are mostly used in symphony orchestras today.

ARGENTINA

The Cowboys of Argentina

In the wide, dusty grasslands of Argentina, a unique group of men called Gauchos once roamed. Important to Argentine culture much in the same way cowboys were to the American wild west, Gauchos are legendary in their own right. They've wandered the Pampas of central Argentina since the 1600s, tending to cattle and protecting ranchers year round.

If you can spot an American cowboy, chances are good that you'd recognize an Argentine Gaucho as well... with just a few differences. Have you ever seen a cowboy with a beret? Called boinas in Spanish, these modern cowboy hats come in every shape and size. In addition, Gauchos wear thick, woolen ponchos in the winter to protect them from the cold. Their interesting geometric patterns make it easy to spot these fellows far off in the distance.

For most of their history, Gauchos have kept to themselves like wild nomads on the vast plains with only their cattle for company. They ate beef roasted over an open fire and drank a strong tea called yerba mate. Although Gauchos still exist today, you'll most likely find them working on a cattle ranch and living as part of the local community.

THIS BAG BELONGS TO

Sun of May
(National symbol of Argentina)
The sun symbol was added to the Argentine flag in 1818 and is inspired by the Incan god Inti.

DESTINATION

Facón: Often the only items a Gaucho owned were the clothes on his back and a decorative knife known as a facón. Used for both protection and as a tool, the knife had a decorative hilt and sheath and could measure up to 20 inches long.

Steak
Chimichurri Pasta

The Spanish Conquistadors are responsible for introducing cattle to Argentina when they were brought over by boat in the early 1500s. Because of the country's perfect environment for raising cattle, beef production in Argentina has become a massive business and a part of the national identity. While many foods might represent Argentine culture, beef is at the top of the list.

Italian
Argentinians

There are more than 24 million Italians living in Argentina, comprising over 44 percent of the immigrant population. Between the 1850s and 1940s, many Italians immigrated to Argentina because of poverty, World Wars I and II and the Great Depression. This explains why Italian culture is so prominent in the country, with pizza, pasta and gelato being some of the country's favorite dishes.

Eva Perón: *(First Lady of Argentina) 1919-1952*
Eva Perón was the spiritual leader of the nation of Argentina and the wife of President Juan Perón. Although she was only 33-years-old when she died, she is remembered as one of the most fascinating women in Argentina's history.

Boleadoras: *Used much in the same manner as a lasso, boleadoras are portions of rope with two ball weights that are used to catch animals such as sheep and cattle.*

Steak Chimichurri Pasta

1 Place all of the chimichurri ingredients in a blender and pulse until all of the large chunks of garlic and parsley are blended nicely.

2 Prepare the steak to your desired level of doneness (stovetop, oven or grill) and set aside for 5 minutes to cool.

3 Lay the asparagus spears in a large skillet filled with 1 inch of water. Bring the water to a simmer, cover and cook for 3 to 5 minutes or until crisp-tender.

4 While the asparagus is simmering, bring a large pot of water to boil over high heat. Add bowtie pasta and cook until al dente (the noodle retaining a bit of its firmness). Drain the noodles and return to the pot.

5 Slice the steak and asparagus into 1-2-inch bite-size pieces. Toss the pasta, chimichurri, steak and asparagus together in the pot. Season with salt and pepper and additional olive oil to taste.

A TIP JUST FOR KIDS

"In Argentina many food items can be ordered *a caballo* which essentially means horseback. Whether you order pizza, pasta or bread, a caballo signifies you'd like a fried egg on top of your meal!"

Ideas for Continued Learning

Celebrate: Search "Argentinian Tango" on Youtube, a special dance originating in Argentina. Learn a step or two and practice at home!

Learn: Argentina is the largest Spanish speaking country in the world. What other countries speak Spanish as their official language?

INGREDIENTS - CHIMICHURRI

2 cloves garlic
1 cup Italian parsley
1/2 cup olive oil
1 teaspoon red wine vinegar
2 tablespoons lemon juice
1/2 teaspoon red pepper flakes
1 teaspoon salt

OTHER INGREDIENTS

16 ounces bowtie pasta
16 ounces flank steak
16 ounces thin asparagus

ARGENTINA

Capital City / Buenos Aires	
Nation Language / Spanish	
Population / 41,660,417	
Currency / Peso	

Argentina is the eighth largest country in the world, with more than one million square miles of land in South America. Argentina is 2,300 miles long from its border with Bolivia in the north to Isla Navarino in the south.

The Mythical Land of Patagonia

When the Spanish explorer Ferdinand Magellan discovered Patagonia in 1520, he started a rumor that persisted for several hundred years. He believed the island was inhabited by giants! Yes, the natives were a little taller than most Europeans, but to call them giants would be exaggerating a bit. Just imagine the tall tales those explorers told their friends and families about the Patagonian giants!

Patagonia is considered the jewel of Argentina, with a richly diverse landscape made up of mountains, rainforests, plains, lakes and rivers. Valued for its natural beauty, Patagonia is home to many unique animals that are not found anywhere else in the world.

Spheniscus Magellanicus
(Magellanic Penguin)

The Magellanic Penguins were discovered by Ferdinand Magellan in 1520 when he spotted millions of the black and white birds around the southern coast of Argentina. Though many of the penguins exist today, they are listed as a threatened species because of damage created by oil spills in the region.

Rhea pennata
(Patagonian Ostrich)

Named after the Greek goddess Rhea, the Patagonian Ostrich is a large flightless bird that can run at speeds up to 37 miles per hour! Now there's a bird you don't want to make enemies with!

Lama guanicoe
(Guanaco)

Living in the mountainous regions of Patagonia, these relatives of the camel can live to be 25 years old. The guanaco are excellent swimmers, and they have adapted to successfully living in rugged terrain where food is sometimes sparse. Their only natural predator is the mountain lion.

Getting to Know Argentina

Fill in the missing information on this page. You can find the correct answers in your copy of *The Cultured Chef,* or search online to retrieve the information needed.

Capital City:

Country Population:

Language:

Google Argentina's flag and use as reference to color the drawing below.

ARGENTINA

Think of Gauchos as very similar to American cowboys. Historically, the Gauchos were ranchers working in the rural regions of Argentina. The traditional Gauchos of the old days are less common, being replaced by common farm hands and laborers. However, the symbol of the Gaucho is important to Argentinian history and culture, and the costumes are worn at special events and celebrations.

SHOPPING FOR A GLOBAL KITCHEN

If you are a young cook and want a little help with some of these activities, you can ask your older brother, sister, neighbor, friend or cousin to help you out. Spending time in the kitchen is always lots of fun, no matter how old you are. If you are a teen-aged chef, consider including a younger chef in these activities as a way to enrich your own experience. You could have a lot more fun teaching or helping youngsters with their first cooking and shopping activities.

Shopping at the International Market

Do you have an international recipe in mind for dinner tonight? If you're looking for recipes that are a little outside your normal eating habits, shop at an ethnic market first for authentic spices and ingredients. Local ethnic grocery stores generally have less expensive prices than supermarkets. And you will most likely discover new foods, meet different people, and benefit your neighborhood economy by shopping locally.

Take your cookbook or your recipes with you. Ask questions about the food and other products at the store. The store clerk will probably have lots of ideas about your recipes and how to help make it very authentic or give it a personal "twist." Plus you could learn a lot of cool things about cultures & cooking!

Shopping at the International Market

"Can you tell me what this ingredient is?"

"What does it taste like?"

"How do you use it?"

"Have you ever made a recipe like this before?"

"How do you pronounce this?"

"Do you have any ideas to help me make this recipe more like something you might make?"

"What is it?"

Visit Your Local Farmer's Market

Visit your local farmers' marketplace. Sure, the farmers in your market are from your own region, but that is exactly what makes it like going to an open-air market or bazaar to pick up your weekly food items. Ours is one of the very few cultures that has large grocery stores where you can purchase everything you need for your home during any given week. The fact is: most other countries have marketplaces where vendors work from stalls every day just like our local farmers do on weekends. We think it's entertainment, but for everyone else around the world, it's a way of life.

BRAZIL

Brazilian Cheese Bread (Pão de Queijo)

This cheese bread recipe is a delicious and extremely popular snack enjoyed throughout much of South America. Pão de Queijo has roots that trace back to Southeastern Brazil, but it should be noted that African slaves are responsible for introducing a similar bread made of Cassava root in the 1800s. Sometime later, someone had the smart idea of adding cheese and making the snack even more delicious!

Toco Toucan - *Ramphastos toco*

Hibiscus - *Hibiscus phoeniceus*

Brazilian Cheese Bread (Pão de Queijo)

1 Preheat oven to 400°F. Coat the mini-muffin tin with olive oil or cooking spray.

2 Put all of the ingredients into a blender and pulse until smooth. If any ingredients fail to blend, while the blender is off, you can use a spatula to push ingredients into the mixture. Continue blending.

3 Pour batter into prepared mini-muffin tin, not quite to the top; leaving about 1/8 inch.

4 Bake at 400°F in the oven for 15-20 minutes, until the tops become golden brown. Remove from the oven and cool. The finished product should be chewy, gooey and delicious.

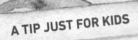

A TIP JUST FOR KIDS

If you'd like to prepare a really authentic meal, serve your Pao de Queijo with rice and beans. You can do a simple Google search for "Brazilian rice and beans recipe" to select a recipe that best meets your needs. You're in for a treat!

Ideas for Continued Learning

Discover: Search "Junior Carnival Brazil" on Youtube and discover the vibrant celebration that takes place each year in Brazil.

Taste: Find a recipe online for "Brazilian Lemonade" and make this beverage for your family and friends. Brazilians refer to this recipe as Swiss Lemonade, but it is served everywhere in Brazil.

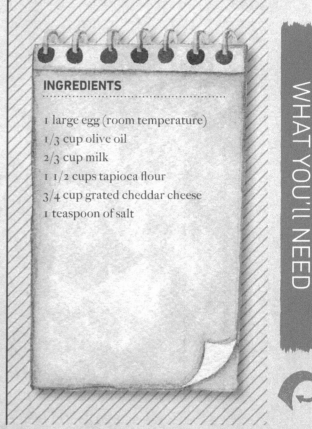

INGREDIENTS

- 1 large egg (room temperature)
- 1/3 cup olive oil
- 2/3 cup milk
- 1 1/2 cups tapioca flour
- 3/4 cup grated cheddar cheese
- 1 teaspoon of salt

BRAZIL

Capital City / Brasília

Nation Language / Portuguese

Population / 210,147,125

Currency / Brazilian Real

Many Portuguese nationals have moved to Brazil over the last few centuries in order to seek economic opportunities. In fact, so many Portuguese moved to Brazil over the years, nearly 20% of all Brazilians have a parent or grandparent from Portugal. (40 million residents)

The Amazon Rainforest

The Amazon River is about 4000 miles long, and spans 2 to 30 miles wide depending upon the season. The canopy of the forest, where the leafy top parts of the trees meet, is so thick it takes nearly ten minutes for water to hit the forest floor when it rains. The forest is home to many strange and exotic plants and animals. There are so many different types of creatures living in the forest that many haven't even been discovered yet.

Interesting Facts about the Amazon Rainforest

• The Amazon Rainforest performs a very important function for humans because it produces nearly 20% of the oxygen on our planet.

• Did you know nearly 60% of the Amazon Rainforest lies within the borders of Brazil? The forest is so large that if it were a country, it would be the 9th largest country in the world.

• The region is home to larger animals as well. Jaguars, howler monkeys, sloths, anacondas, alligators and capybara also live there.

• The Amazon River is nearly 3,977 miles long, and at its widest point it can be 6.8 miles wide during the dry season. There are no bridges spanning the Amazon anywhere, along the entire path of the river.

Sloth - Bradypus variegatus

Getting to Know Brazil

Fill in the missing information on this page. You can find the correct answers in your copy of *The Cultured Chef*, or search online to retrieve the information needed.

Capital City:

Country Population:

Language:

....

Google Brazil's flag and use as reference to color the drawing below.

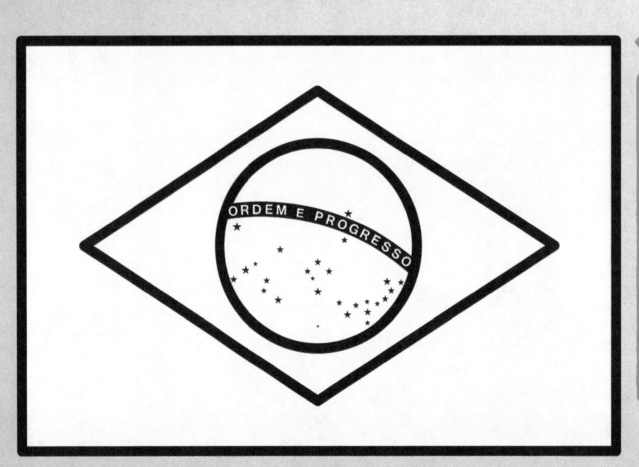

BRAZIL

Brazil - Carnival Celebration

Carnival is a religious celebration that takes place all over the word. In Brazil, Samba dancers wear vibrant costumes with flashy accessories as they perform in parades.

THE INTERNATIONAL PANTRY

When you decide that you want to try to cook some of the foods that your friends from other countries have grown up eating, you will need to have a few of the ingredients from those cultures and recipes on hand in your kitchen.

Because our American culture is becoming more globally aware all the time, a lot of the ingredients in the recipes of this cookbook can be found at your neighborhood grocery store. Even though these ingredients are organized by the cultures in this section, lots of foods, spices, and herbs are used across many different cultures.

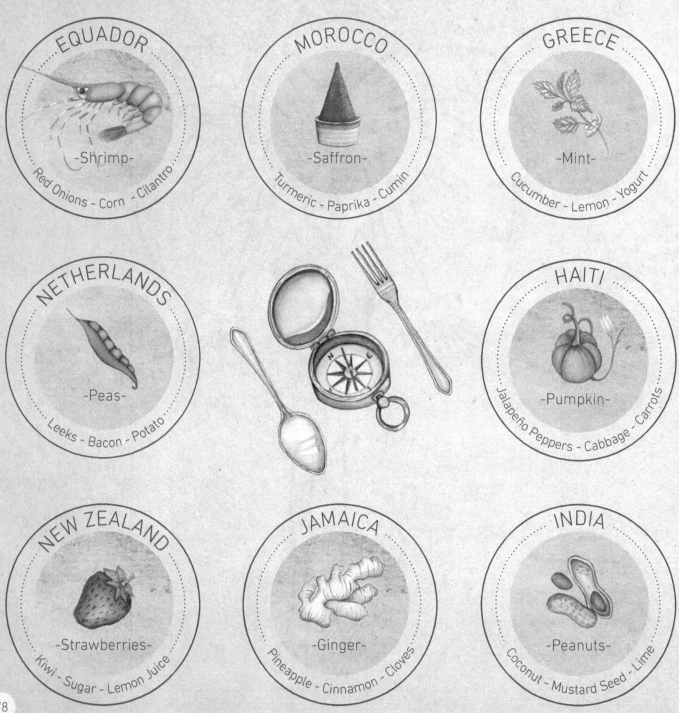

EQUADOR
-Shrimp-
Red Onions - Corn - Cilantro

MOROCCO
-Saffron-
Turmeric - Paprika - Cumin

GREECE
-Mint-
Cucumber - Lemon - Yogurt

NETHERLANDS
-Peas-
Leeks - Bacon - Potato

HAITI
-Pumpkin-
Jalapeño Peppers - Cabbage - Carrots

NEW ZEALAND
-Strawberries-
Kiwi - Sugar - Lemon Juice

JAMAICA
-Ginger-
Pineapple - Cinnamon - Cloves

INDIA
-Peanuts-
Coconut - Mustard Seed - Lime

Colombia

Arepas

Arepas are round, flat, slightly thick, corn flour disks that can be used as a base for piling ingredients on top of, or they can be sliced down the center and used like two slices of bread with ingredients piled in between the slices. Arepas are a very important part of Colombian cuisine, consumed in almost every household.

Don't be afraid to be adventurous with your Arepas. You can serve them at breakfast with cheese, potatoes and eggs. Try them with shredded chicken, or you can make a vegetarian snack!

Common Squirrel Monkey - *Saimiri sciureus*

Arepas

1 Mix together the arepa flour, cheese, and salt in a bowl, then stir in the water until it's mixed well. Let the ingredients sit until enough water is absorbed for a soft dough to form. That should only take 1 to 2 minutes.

2 Form 3 tablespoons of dough into a single ball and flatten between your palms, patting and gently pressing until you form a 1/4-inch-thick patty (2 1/2 to 3 inches wide). Gently press around the side of the disk so you can get rid of any cracks that form in the dough. Set the patty on a wax-paper-lined surface. Continue forming and setting aside more disks until you run out of dough.

3 Heat oil in a large nonstick skillet over medium heat. When the oil begins to shimmer, fry arepas in batches, turning over once, until the disks become golden brown. This should take about 8 to 10 minutes per batch. Pat dry with paper towels.

A TIP JUST FOR KIDS

Whistle while you work! Check out the folk music of Rafael Escalona while you prepare your arepas. You can find music for free on Youtube, or download on iTunes if you'd like. His traditional accordion and guitar music will help you enjoy a lively meal.

Ideas for Continued Learning

Watch: Look up videos or photos "Caño Cristales," or The River of Five Colors. It is one of the most beautiful rivers in the world.

Discover: Colombia is one of the most bio-diverse countries in the world. Write a list of some of the plant and animal species that are native to Colombia.

INGREDIENTS

1 cup arepa flour
  (precooked cornmeal) available in
  the global foods section of most
  markets
1 cup grated mozzarella
1 cup water
1/4 cup vegetable oil
1/8 teaspoon salt

COLOMBIA

Capital City / Bogotá	
Nation Language / Spanish	
Population / 48,258,494	
Currency / Colombian Peso	

Cano Cristales (The River of Five Colors) is located in the center of Colombia. The river is unique because aquatic plants growing on the riverbed change colors between yellow, red, blue, green and black from July through November, creating a kaleidoscope of colors. Google this phenomenon for more information.

The Legend of El Dorado

The Muisca are an indigenous people and culture dating back long before the Spanish conquest in the 1500s. They were one of the four advanced civilizations of the Americas which included the Aztec, Maya and Inca. The Legend of El Dorado originates from stories about a mythical Muisca tribal chief, and a hidden city of gold.

The possibility of finding or confiscating gold has fueled wars and expeditions for many thousands of years. In fact, gold played a large part in the Spanish Conquest of the indigenous populations in the Americas. One myth, in particular, led Spanish explorers to the Andes in what is now Colombia. As the story goes, when a new chief rose to power in the community, they would cover him in gold dust. They would throw the gold and precious jewels into Lake Guatavita to find favor with a god that lived underwater.

The legend of this golden chief spread when explorers started calling him El Dorado, meaning "The Gilded One." Explorers were finding gold elsewhere, so it wasn't a stretch of the imagination that they would find more gold high in the Andes. The famous explorer Sir Walter Raleigh traveled to the region twice in search of the splendor, but he came up relatively empty-handed.

Did this city of gold with the golden chief really exist? Edgar Allan Poe gave us a clue in 1849 when he wrote, "Over the Mountains of the Moon, down the Valley of the Shadow, ride, boldly ride... if you seek for El Dorado."

Guanaco -
Lama guanicoe

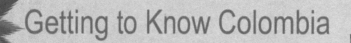

Fill in the missing information on this page. You can find the correct answers in your copy of *The Cultured Chef*, or search online to retrieve the information needed.

Capital City:

Country Population:

Language:

Google Colombia's flag and use as reference to color the drawing below.

COLOMBIA

Colombia

One of the most spectaclar religious sites in Colombia is the Santuario de Las Lajas, built on a bridge spanning the Guaitara River. The amazing structure looks like it is straight from a fairy tale.

The Flora and Fauna of South America

South America is Earth's fourth largest continent. The Amazon River runs through South America and is surrounded by the largest and one of the most important rainforests in the world. The continent has jungles, deserts and mountain ranges. There are even some glaciers in the south!

Animals
of South America

There is a lot to consider when learning about animals of the world. Different animals are suited to different climates, and have particular tastes when it comes to the food they need to survive. A penguin won't feel very much at home on the beach in Miami, Florida, would it?

Select an animal from the previous page about South America and write a short report below. Where does the animal live? What does the animal like to eat? Are there any other facts about this animal you find interesting?

Use the space below to write down interesting facts about the animal you have chosen.

SOUTH AMERICA

"*Healthy citizens are the greatest asset any country can have.*"

British Prime Minister, Winston Churchill

EUROPE

SCOTLAND - RUSSIA - HUNGARY - PORTUGAL - GERMANY - FRANCE - SWEDEN - POLAND - NETHERLANDS - GREECE - ITALY

Scotland

The National Symbol of Scotland

The unicorn, believe it or not, is the national animal of Scotland. It has long stood as a symbol of the region, appearing on the royal coat of arms as early as the 1600s. But, you may still be wondering why an imaginary animal is the symbol for such a great nation.

Unicorns are fascinating characters in literary history and oral traditions in Europe. Although they are remarkably beautiful and elegant, they are also depicted as being extremely fierce, proud and unpredictable creatures. Stories often involve unicorns fighting to the death rather than experiencing slavery in captivity.

The Scottish people have come to feel a sort of kinship with the mythical creature as they've struggled to retain their freedom over the years. Represented in great works of art, tapestries hanging in royal palaces and even gold coins and currencies, the unicorn has found a special place in the hearts of the people of Scotland.

Everyone has a weakness. Only young maidens have the ability to tame wild unicorns. Stories claim the only unicorns ever to be caught were found because they fell asleep with their heads rested on the laps of young girls napping in the woods.

Scottish Thistle - *Silybum marianum*

The Scottish Thistle

According to an ancient legend, Norse armies were invading Scotland many years ago. In the middle of the night when the Scottish army was fast asleep, a barefoot Norseman approaching their camp stepped on a thistle and cried out in pain. This alerted the Scottish army who woke from their sleep to defeat the invading army. Since then, the thistle has been become a symbol of nobility and Scottish heritage.

Shortbread Cookies

With only four ingredients, shortbread is quite possibly one of the simplest recipes you can make in the kitchen. However, it has anything but a simple history. The national dish has been prepared for royalty and nobility since the 12th century. Prestigious monarchs such as Mary, Queen of Scots and Queen Victoria referred to it as their favorite dessert — a required dish in their households for both Christmas and Scottish New Year.

In the 12th century, shortbread was a little different. Historically, the word "biscuit" meant twice-baked bread. Bakers would collect all the extra pieces of dough after making bread, and send it to the oven a second time to form hard, dry rounds of bread. Over time, butter was added to the recipe making it more of a commodity for people who could afford the nicer things in life. The large amount of butter in shortbread makes it the crispy and crumbly dessert we know today.

Adopted in the 12th century by William I, who was known as "William the Lion," the Red Lion has since become a national symbol of Scotland.

Shortbread Cookies

1 Preheat the oven to 325 degrees Fahrenheit.

2 Sift the flour through a sieve into a small bowl. Set aside.

3 In a large bowl, cream together the butter, sugar and orange extract. Add the flour. Mix well. You may have to use your hands toward the end to get the mixture to form a ball.

4 Flatten the ball onto waxed or parchment paper and roll into a ½-inch thick rectangle. Use a small cookie cutter to cut out 2-inch squares. Place ½-inch apart on a parchment lined cookie sheet.

5 Bake for 14-16 minutes or until bottoms are light golden brown. Do not over bake.

6 In small bowl, microwave chocolate chips and shortening on High 1 to 1 1/2 minutes or until melted; stir until smooth. Once the shortbread has cooled, dip a portion of each cookie into the melted chocolate. Place on waxed paper until chocolate is set.

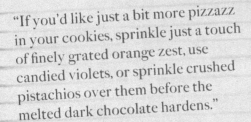

A TIP JUST FOR KIDS!

"If you'd like just a bit more pizzazz in your cookies, sprinkle just a touch of finely grated orange zest, use candied violets, or sprinkle crushed pistachios over them before the melted dark chocolate hardens."

Ideas for Continued Learning

Learn: Mary Stuart, or Mary Queen of Scots, is a fascinating historical figure. Learn more about this queen who spent over 18 years under house arrest by Queen Elizabeth I of England.

Discover: The Highland Games are Scotland's way of celebrating their unique sporting culture and traditions. Learn more about this annual celebration.

INGREDIENTS

- 1 cup unsalted butter
- 3/4 cup powdered sugar
- 1 tablespoon orange extract
- 2 1/2 cups all-purpose flour
- 1 cup semisweet chocolate chips
- 2 tablespoons shortening

SCOTLAND

Capital City / Edinburgh	
Nation Language / English	
Population / 5,313,600	
Currency / Pound sterling	

Scotland *is located in Europe and comprises the upper third of Great Britain. Forming a great peninsula, Scotland is surrounded by water on three sides: the Atlantic Ocean, the North Sea and the Irish Sea.*

The Loch Ness Monster

A cryptid is the name of an animal whose existence has not been authenticated by the scientific community. We've heard of many cryptids in our time, including Bigfoot, the Abominable Snowman and of course the Loch Ness Monster.

There are few people in the world who haven't heard about the Loch Ness Monster of Scotland. The Loch Ness monster, or Nessie for short, is reported to be living in the profoundly deep body of water called Loch Ness. This vast body of water was created many years ago when a massive tremor caused the earth to open up along the Great Glen fault line. The Loch is reported to be 754 feet deep and two and a half miles long, with a bottom as flat as the playing field of a football stadium. All of this creates an environment perfectly suited for a giant sea monster!

Nessie has been sighted many times in the last 100 years by fisherman, residents and even tourists. However, no one has been able to provide conclusive evidence in the form of video footage, photos or tissue samples that would convince scientists the animal really exists. However, ask anyone living in the area surrounding the Loch; everyone has a story or knows someone who has a story about Nessie. She makes for an interesting legend, indeed.

What to look for:

Nessie has been described as anywhere from 18-50 feet long and greyish-black to dark brown in color. She has a barrel-shaped body and looks like the prehistoric plesiosaur. (An aquatic reptile that went extinct 65 million years ago)

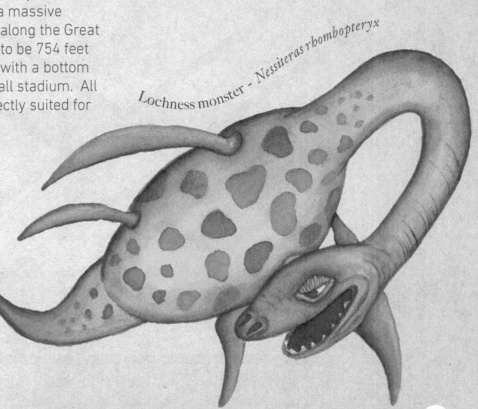

Lochness monster - *Nessiteras rhombopteryx*

Getting to Know Scotland

Fill in the missing information on this page. You can find the correct answers in your copy of *The Cultured Chef,* or search online to retrieve the information needed.

Capital City:

Country Population:

Language:

Google Scotland's flag and use as reference to color the drawing below.

SCOTLAND

The bagpipe is the national instrument of Scotland and is famous all over the world as a symbol of the country. The instrument has a long history dating back to ancient origins.

MASKS OF THE WORLD

Masks have been a part of important rituals and ceremonies in every corner of the globe since prehistoric times. Created from nearly every material known to man, ceremonial masks come in every shape, color and size. Depending on the culture, some masks are even thought to possess a power or magic of their own. Can you think of any occasions when we might wear masks in our culture?

AFRICA

Many African tribes feel it is easier for animals to communicate with spirits than man. Thus, animals are often incorporated into ceremonial mask designs. This West-African mask is carved out of teak, a hardwood regularly used for making masks.

TIBET

This ceremonial mask was used in the 17th century in northern Tibet. The mask depicts Garuda, a powerful bird found in Buddhist mythology. Garuda is a powerful antidote against the negative influence of nagas "spirits," which the Tibetans believed might be responsible for illness and bad luck.

Peru

Celebrated in Bolivia and Peru, Danza de los Diablos "Dance of the Devils" features performers dressed in devil masks and costumes. Stylistically, the masks range from simple to incredibly ornate designs.

Green Man

Stemming from European folklore and pagan beliefs, the Green Man is a god who represents the spirits of the trees, plants and foliage. Depictions of the Green Man have been found in medieval art throughout Europe as well as great literary works such as Sir Gawain and the Green Knight.

Yu'pik

The central Alaskan Yup'ik people are a nomadic indigenous tribe living in western and southwestern Alaska. More than 22,000 members of the tribe exist today, and they continue to practice their traditional mask making. Once a mask is used for a ceremonial dance, it is destroyed and never used again.

Sri Lanka

Created by the native Sinhalese people of Sri Lanka, a mask of this nature is created to provide peace, harmony and wealth. Legend has it the country was once ruled by a mythical people called Raksasas. Although the Raksha people are long gone and may have never existed at all, their masks are still worn during traditional Sri Lankan dances. The fanciful blue creature in this mask is named Mayura, a peacock who provides transport for the Buddhist god Ceylon.

Italy

Medico della Peste

Based on a traditional Venetian Carnival design, the Medico della Peste (Plague Doctor Mask) wasn't originally intended for parties. It had a far more practical application and was used by doctors during the plague to prevent the spread of disease.

Carnival of Venice

Carnival in Venice is one of the crown jewels of Italian culture. Stepping off a gondola onto the city's cobblestone streets during Carnival is like walking into a fairy tale. The great city comes alive, bursting forth in bright colors, sequins and feathers, all belonging to a unique cast of costumed characters roaming the streets. The Venetian Carnival is one of the most unique celebrations in the world.

Almost every culture celebrates some version of Carnival, but in Italy the tradition is uniquely tied to the Catholic season of Lent. The faithful churchgoers are required to fast (to not eat certain foods) for six weeks prior to Easter every year. Thus, Carnival represents the final opportunity to indulge in the luxuries of expensive food and wine before the fast begins.

Olive Branch - *Olea europaea*

Referred to as il Tricolore, the colors of the Italian flag are said to represent hope (green), faith (white) and charity (red).

" *Passami l'olio, per favore!* "

Caprese Salad
(Insalata Caprese)

Nothing is more enjoyable on a hot summer afternoon than a plate of Caprese Salad with tasty red tomatoes, fresh mozzarella and basil just picked from the garden! Chances are you've had this delicious treat before, but do you know its history?

There is a lot of mystery surrounding the creator of Italy's favorite salad, but we know one thing for sure; it was first seen on the menu at Quisisana Hotel on the Island of Capri in 1920, just after World War One. Most likely, a very patriotic cook whipped up this salad for the first time in honor of his country. The Caprese Salad is comprised of the colors of the Italian national flag, green, white and red.

Caprese Salad (Insalata Caprese)

1 Wash the tomatoes and basil. Assemble a cherry tomato, mozzarella ball and basil leaf for every skewer you want to make.

2 Insert the skewer through the tomato, basil and mozzarella, positioning the items securely, and leaving room to pick up the skewer later.

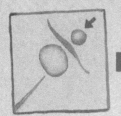

3 Assemble the Caprese skewers on a plate and drizzle lightly with olive oil.

4 Season with salt and pepper to taste.

5 To make a balsamic glaze, in a small pan, heat one cup of balsamic vinegar over medium-low heat. Stirring occasionally, allow the vinegar to come to a very gentle simmer. Cook for 10 minutes until the mixture becomes syrupy in consistency. Be careful not to burn the vinegar. Allow the glaze to cool, then drizzle on top of your skewers.

A TIP JUST FOR KIDS!

"If you'd like to make a more portable version of Caprese, you can assemble and shake up all the ingredients in a medium size container with a lid. It makes an easy snack to take to a picnic, dinner at a friend's house or any special event."

Ideas for Continued Learning

Experience: Mosaic art has been celebrated in Italy for many thousands of years. Do a Google image search of "Italian Mosaic Art" and view some of the beautiful works of art.

Discover: Italy loves opera! Listen to "O mio babbino caro" on youtube and share how you feel about this kind of music.

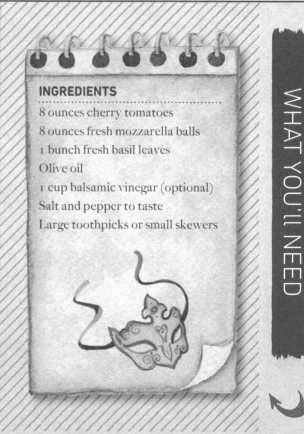

INGREDIENTS

8 ounces cherry tomatoes

8 ounces fresh mozzarella balls

1 bunch fresh basil leaves

Olive oil

1 cup balsamic vinegar (optional)

Salt and pepper to taste

Large toothpicks or small skewers

ITALY

Capital City /	Rome
Nation Language /	Italian
Population /	61,482,297
Currency /	Euro

Italy is a long and narrow peninsula in southern Europe surrounded by the Mediterranean Sea. The country is famously shaped like a high-heeled boot kicking a ball, which is the Italian island of Sicily.

The Gondoliers of Venice

Did you know the entire city of Venice was built on a series of small islands and marshlands off the coast of Italy? The muddy coastal waters provided a safe haven from invaders hoping to steal the riches of the wealthy merchants that lived there. But the question was, how do you build a great city on the water? The Venetian founders needed to think a little differently. They drove great wooden spikes down into the thick mud to create foundations for their homes. And instead of regular paved streets, they created a series of waterways called canals.

Rarely is there a postcard of Italy that doesn't include scenes from beautiful Venice. A city unlike any other in the world, Venice is magical. Visitors from all over the world descend upon Italy to experience the wonder of Venice for themselves. The canals are full of boats traveling in every direction, carrying tourists and locals alike.

Just like a big city needs taxis and taxi drivers, Venice needs gondolas and gondoliers. A gondola is like a water taxi, and a gondolier is a specially trained person who propels and steers the gondola along the narrow and busy canals throughout the city. The city of Venice limits the number of gondolier licenses to 450, which makes for fierce competition when a gondolier dies. To make things more interesting, a gondolier can pass his license on to his son when he retires or dies.

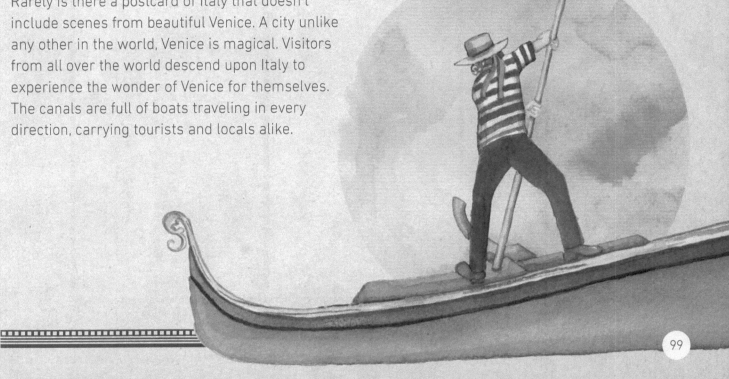

Getting to Know Italy

Fill in the missing information on this page. You can find the correct answers in your copy of *The Cultured Chef*, or search online to retrieve the information needed.

SIGHTSEEING

Capital City:

Country Population:

Language:

Google Italy's flag and use as reference to color the drawing below.

ITALY

Italy

The Lion of Venice is an ancient bronze
winged lion sculpture located in Piazza San Marco
in Venice, Italy. The sculpture dates back to 300 BCE,
and has come to be seen as the symbol
of Venice. Variations of the lion can be
found depicted throughout the city.

GREECE

Ancient Greece

Many of the crowning achievements of Western civilization can be traced back to the ancient Greeks who prospered during the Classical period of 500-336 BC. Many important ideas about medicine, government, theatre, art and architecture were birthed during this time. The list of achievements during the period is endless, with many modern conveniences such as the alarm clock, the shower, vending machines and umbrellas invented due to Greek discoveries.

Aesop's Fables

The collection of tales we know as Aesop's Fables have been enjoyed by children and adults alike for more than 2,000 years. Perhaps you've heard some of the stories? The Boy Who Cried Wolf, The Tortoise and the Hare, The Goose that Laid the Golden Egg, and the Lion and the Mouse are all stories told by a man named Aesop (620-560 BC).

There is a lot of debate over details about Aesop's life. He has been depicted as both a dwarf with a crooked nose and bent back as well as a black man from Ethiopia. What we know for sure is that Aesop's fables have influenced millions of readers and provided inspiration for many popular children's books today.

Hippocrates

80 ΕΛΛΑΣ

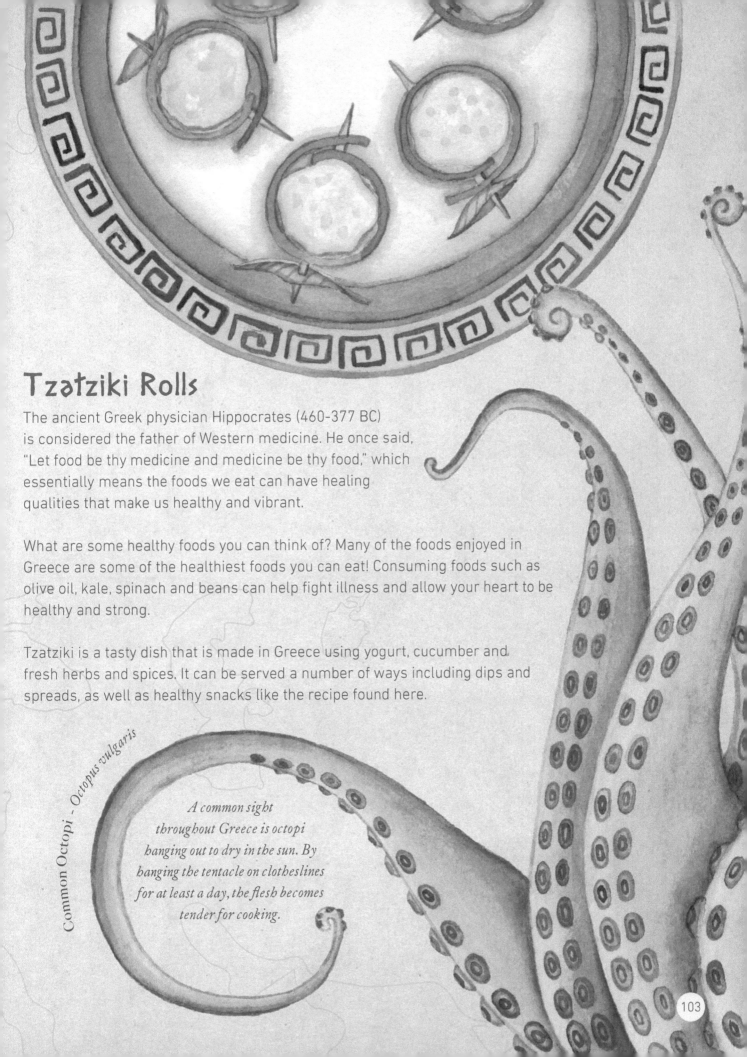

Tzatziki Rolls

The ancient Greek physician Hippocrates (460-377 BC) is considered the father of Western medicine. He once said, "Let food be thy medicine and medicine be thy food," which essentially means the foods we eat can have healing qualities that make us healthy and vibrant.

What are some healthy foods you can think of? Many of the foods enjoyed in Greece are some of the healthiest foods you can eat! Consuming foods such as olive oil, kale, spinach and beans can help fight illness and allow your heart to be healthy and strong.

Tzatziki is a tasty dish that is made in Greece using yogurt, cucumber and fresh herbs and spices. It can be served a number of ways including dips and spreads, as well as healthy snacks like the recipe found here.

Common Octopi - Octopus vulgaris

A common sight throughout Greece is octopi hanging out to dry in the sun. By hanging the tentacle on clotheslines for at least a day, the flesh becomes tender for cooking.

Tzatziki Rolls

1 Cut the ends off the English cucumbers and slice lengthwise at about 1/8 inch thickness. Note: You'll want the strips of cucumber to be thin enough they can be flexible, but thick enough that they won't fall apart.

2 Lightly sprinkle salt over each side of the cucumber strips and leave them for 10 minutes.

3 In a small mixing bowl, stir in the yogurt, lemon juice, garlic cloves, dill and mint until evenly mixed.

4 Rinse the cucumber strips and pat them dry using a paper towel.

5 Lay the cucumber strip flat, spoon a small scoop of yogurt mixture at the end of the cucumber strip and roll using a toothpick to hold the strip and mint garnish in place. Repeat until mixture runs out.

A TIP JUST FOR KIDS

"If you don't want to make rolls, try making little cucumber sandwiches by slicing the cucumbers into coins instead. Place a layer of yogurt mix between two cucumber coins to form a little sandwich! Or use the coins like chips to dip into the yogurt mixture."

Ideas for Continued Learning

Research: Thira (otherwise known as Santorini) is a world famous Greek island, known for its beautiful architecture. Research this island and tell someone what you learned.

Taste: Dolmas are a traditional snack of stuffed grape leaves in Greece. Find some at your local market and see how you like them.

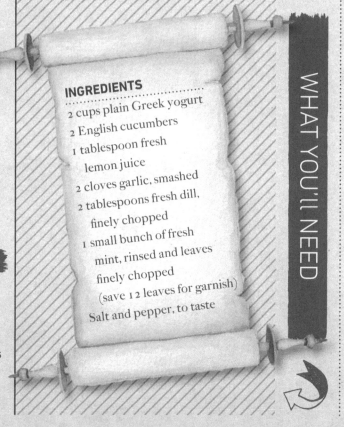

INGREDIENTS

2 cups plain Greek yogurt

2 English cucumbers

1 tablespoon fresh lemon juice

2 cloves garlic, smashed

2 tablespoons fresh dill, finely chopped

1 small bunch of fresh mint, rinsed and leaves finely chopped (save 12 leaves for garnish)

Salt and pepper, to taste

GREECE

Capital City / Athens	
Nation Language / Greek	
Population / 10,772,967	
Currency / Euro	

Greece *is comprised of a mainland peninsula and an astounding 1,400 islands scattered throughout the Mediterranean Sea. Only 169 of the islands actually have people living on them, the largest two being Crete and Euboea.*

Zeus, the King of Greek Mythology

Have you ever wondered why good and bad things happen and why you don't seem to have much control over those events? The ancient Greeks had those thoughts as well, and they answered their questions by telling stories about an enchanted family of gods who ruled heaven and earth.

The stories the ancient Greeks told have become known as mythology. Their stories explained the nature of people and science and helped them understand life in general. Because they believed the gods could directly affect the lives of humans, it was important to know the personalities and characteristics of each of the gods so they wouldn't unknowingly offend them.

Zeus was the king of all the gods and the father of all men. More powerful than any other gods, he could throw his voice, shape shift and toss lightning bolts through the sky at wrongdoers. He is represented as the god of mercy and justice, the protector of the meek and the punisher of the unjust.

Getting to Know Greece

Fill in the missing information on this page. You can find the correct answers in your copy of *The Cultured Chef,* or search online to retrieve the information needed.

Capital City:

Country Population:

Language:

....

Google Greece's flag and use as reference to color the drawing below.

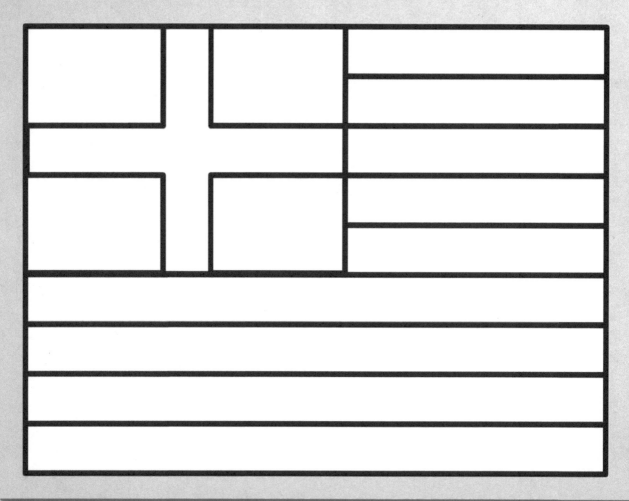

GREECE

Color the World!

Greece

The Laurel wreath has become a symbol
of ancient Greece and the Olympic Games
that were created there. The wreath was given
to winners of competions. The wreath also appears
in Greek Mythology, being worn by the god Apollo.

HOUSES OF THE WORLD

Not everyone lives in a wooden house with three bedrooms, two bathrooms and a kitchen. In fact, the traditional American home is far from the norm in places like Guatemala where a home is usually one or two rooms with a dirt floor. When reviewing the homes in this section, consider why each home is built the way it is. What is the weather like in the region? What is the economic situation? Learning about homes around the world provides a wonderful glimpse into life in other countries.

Jabu: In North Sumatra, Indonesia, the Batak Toba people live in wooden boat-like structures on stilts called jabu. With a high thatched roof and only one small window on each side, the home stays pretty dark inside, making it a great place to sleep. Families who live in a jabu spend most of their time outside.

Beehive Houses: the heat in the Middle East can be incredibly difficult to bear, therefore Syrian beehive houses use natural elements such as mud, dirt, straw and stones to better protect themselves from the heat. Syrian homes in this style have been continuously built since 3700 BC.

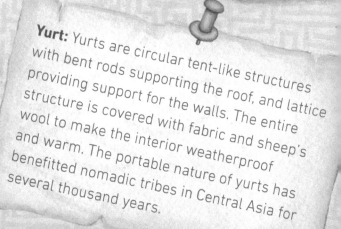

Yurt: Yurts are circular tent-like structures with bent rods supporting the roof, and lattice structure is covered with fabric and sheep's wool to make the interior weatherproof and warm. The portable nature of yurts has benefitted nomadic tribes in Central Asia for several thousand years.

Turf Houses: Turf homes in Iceland have been built for over 1,000 years as a way of dealing with the difficult and cold climate. First a flat stone foundation is laid out, then a traditional wooden structure with a steep-pitched roof is built. Finally, the house is surrounded and topped with turf (grass with dirt and roots attached) that acts as insulation.

Igloo: The igloo is a home built out of blocks of ice and snow and is primarily used by the Inuit people (commonly known as Eskimo) in Canada and parts of Alaska. Even in temperatures well below zero, the igloo can maintain a temperature of 19 to 60 degrees Fahrenheit based solely on the body heat created by the people sleeping inside.

Adobe: The adobe homes of Guatemala are made from mud and straw bricks that are baked in the sun then stacked to create a traditional house with four walls. The structures usually have a tile or tin roof. Homes like these can be found in all parts of Mexico and Central America and are usually painted in an assortment of bright colors.

Netherlands

Enough Windmills to go Around

It is almost impossible to think of the Netherlands without picturing Dutch scenes of windmills and tulips. But why are these two items so important to Dutch culture? The people of the Netherlands have had a long and constant struggle to create usable, dry land for settling and farming. They have used windmills to pump water since the 14th century, using as many as ten thousand windmills at any one time. Although only one thousand or so of these majestic structures exist today, they still make for an incredible sight!

Tulips: Worth Their Weight In Gold

In the late 1500s, the kings and queens of Europe saw tulips as a status symbol, and the brightly colored flowers were in incredible demand. Today a tulip bulb can be purchased for as little as $0.25, but in the 1600s it could sell for ten times what an average person earned in a year! With that kind of popularity, tulips required acres and acres of land, and the Netherlands was the perfect place for growing, with its mild climate and wet springs.

Klompen are wooden shoes (or clogs) used by Dutch farmers and gardeners and adored by tourists. The old-fashioned shoes are so popular that nearly three million pairs are manufactured each year.

Dutch Pea Soup "Snert" (Erwtensoep)

What comes to mind when you hear the word "Snert"? Would you ever guess that it's the name for a delicious bacon and pea soup from the Netherlands? The Dutch have been preparing Snert for a long time, often enjoying a bowl during the long, cold winter months.

Although the Dutch perfected it, pea soup has been around for a really long time. The Greek playwright Aristophanes referred to it in his play "The Birds" around the year 400 BC because it was commonly sold in the markets of Athens. In fact, this dish is so popular you can find references to it in almost every culture around the world. You may have heard the famous poem from England that reads, "Pease porridge hot, Pease porridge cold, Pease porridge in the pot, Nine days old."

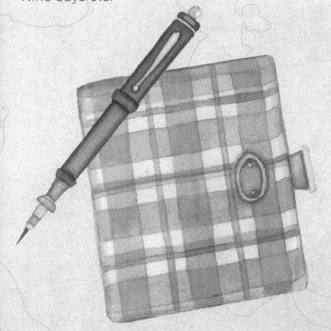

Anne Frank: The Diary of a Young Girl

Anne Frank might be one of the most famous fifteen-year-olds the world has ever known. When she died in March 1945, one of the many Jewish victims of the Holocaust, she left behind a journal detailing her family's struggles to hide during the German occupation of the Netherlands. It has since become one of the most widely read journals in the world, giving readers worldwide a glimpse into war and its impact on human life. Anne's diary has been printed in 50 languages and has sold more than 25 million copies.

Go to AnneFrank.org to find out more about this amazing young woman.

111

Snert (Erwtensoep)

1 In a medium size pan, bring split peas, chicken broth, pork chop and bacon to a boil. Be sure to remove any froth that forms on top of the mixture. Place a lid over the pan and leave to simmer on low heat for 45 minutes. Stir often, making sure to prevent the ingredients from sticking to the bottom of the pan.

2 Take the pork chop and bacon out, debone and cut all the meat thinly. Set aside.

3 Add the onion, leek, carrot, celery, celery root and potato to the split pea mixture. Allow to boil for another 30 minutes.

4 When the vegetables become fork tender, puree half of the mixture in a blender. Return the blended material as well as the pork chop and bacon to the pot and mix well. If you like your soup chunky, puree only a quarter of the soup mixture.

5 Dice the kielbasa and mix with the soup several minutes before serving.

A TIP JUST FOR KIDS

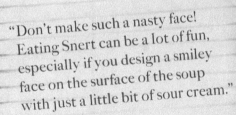

"Don't make such a nasty face! Eating Snert can be a lot of fun, especially if you design a smiley face on the surface of the soup with just a little bit of sour cream."

Ideas for Continued Learning

Consider: Bicycles are the primary mode of transportation in Amsterdam. Discover the other methods of transport in Amsterdam, and then do the same for your own city. What benefits are there in taking alternative forms of transportation?

INGREDIENTS

11 ounces dried split peas

4 cups chicken stock

1 pork chop, 6 ounces

4 ounces bacon (or 6 slices)

1 small onion, finely diced

4 ounces leeks, finely diced

4 ounces carrots, diced

4 ounces celery root (leave it out if you can't find it)

1 large potato, peeled and diced

2 stalks celery, chopped

Optional: 1, 14-ounce kielbasa, diced

NETHERLANDS

| Capital City / Amsterdam |
| Nation Language / Dutch |
| Population / 16,788,973 |
| Currency / Euro |

The Netherlands *is situated in a flat region of Europe where most of the land lies below sea level. It is reported that more than 65 percent of the country would be under water if it weren't for nearly 1,500 miles of dykes that prevent the North Sea from flooding the country.*

Vincent van Gogh

The Netherlands has had its fair share of famous artists. The 17th century was known as "The Age of the Dutch Masters" when the region claimed many important painters including Rembrandt and Vermeer.

Vincent van Gogh is one of the most famous Dutch artists, known both for his post-impressionistic style and his wild bouts of anxiety and depression. Deeply troubled his entire life, van Gogh channeled his passion and anxiety through his work. Take a moment to do a web search on Vincent van Gogh and get to know his paintings. It's likely that you've already seen a van Gogh painting without realizing it was his.

Among van Gogh's most famous paintings is The Starry Night. The night landscape in this painting comes to life with stars and light swirling and dancing off the page. How does it make you feel to know the artist painted this masterpiece while he was under considerable stress? Though van Gogh only lived to be 37, he left behind a wealth of material with more than 2,100 works of art.

"Starry Night"

Getting to Know Netherlands

Fill in the missing information on this page. You can find the correct answers in your copy of *The Cultured Chef*, or search online to retrieve the information needed.

Capital City:

Country Population:

Language:

Google the Netherlands flag and use as reference to color the drawing below.

Netherlands - Tulips and Windmills

If you travel to the Netherlands in the spring, your vacation wouldn't be complete without a trip to the countryside where tulip farms and windmills dot the landscape. The region offers the perfect growing conditions for spring flowering bulbs, so many varieties are grown there.

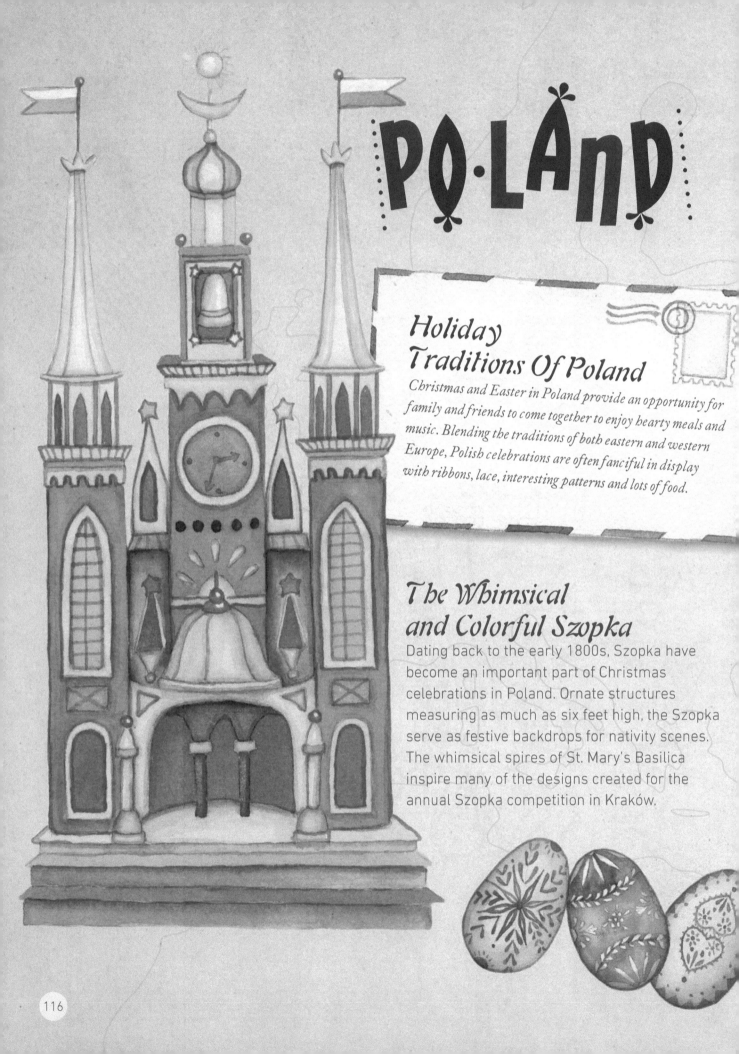

PO·LAND

Holiday Traditions Of Poland

Christmas and Easter in Poland provide an opportunity for family and friends to come together to enjoy hearty meals and music. Blending the traditions of both eastern and western Europe, Polish celebrations are often fanciful in display with ribbons, lace, interesting patterns and lots of food.

The Whimsical and Colorful Szopka

Dating back to the early 1800s, Szopka have become an important part of Christmas celebrations in Poland. Ornate structures measuring as much as six feet high, the Szopka serve as festive backdrops for nativity scenes. The whimsical spires of St. Mary's Basilica inspire many of the designs created for the annual Szopka competition in Kraków.

Polanaise is the name of a special Polish dance performed as an opening event of a Studniówka (Polish high school prom). This event takes place one hundred days before final exams.

Angel Wings
(Chrusciki)

These delicious dessert items have enjoyed widespread appeal throughout history. They are available in many countries worldwide, and each region offers its own traditions and local names. Light and crispy with a dusting of powdered sugar, Angel Wings are enjoyed in Polish households during Easter and other special occasions. They truly are the perfect treat for any special event.

A Good Egg

Pisanki (Painted Polish Eggs) have been an important part of the Polish Easter celebrations for over a thousand years. The beautiful designs are created by first dipping an egg into hot wax, which forms a seal around it. After the wax hardens, an ornate design is scratched into it and then the egg is dipped into dye. The dye only adheres to the egg where the wax has been removed, creating a beautiful pattern.

What's In a Name?

In the United States they're known as Angel Wings, but in Poland they're known as Chrusciki. Depending upon whom you ask, the word means broken, dry twigs or brushwood. That makes sense if you think about it. Imagine walking through the ancient Białowieża Forest in Poland, and hearing the sound of dry twigs crackling and breaking under your feet. That's exactly what eating an Angel Wing sounds like!

117

Angel Wings (Chrusciki)

1 In a medium size mixing bowl, cut butter into the flour until the mixture resembles coarse crumbs.

2 In a separate bowl, beat egg yolks with the sour cream and vanilla. Add to flour mixture, mix, then refrigerate overnight.

3 Preheat oven to 350 degrees Fahrenheit. Roll dough out to ¼ inch thickness on a flat surface. Cut into 1½-inch by 3-inch rectangles.

4 Make a 1-inch slit centered into each rectangle. Pull a corner through to make a bowtie or angel wing.

5 Place Angel Wings 1-inch apart on a parchment lined baking sheet, bake for 7-10 minutes or until golden brown. Sprinkle with powdered sugar when cool.

A TIP JUST FOR KIDS!

"Chrusciki are typically deep fried in oil or lard in order to get their trademark crispiness. If you're looking for an absolutely traditional experience, feel free to Google "Chrusciki Recipe" in order to find a recipe for the fried version."

INGREDIENTS

2 cups flour

1/2 cup sour cream

1/2 cup sugar

3 egg yolks

1/2 pound butter

1 teaspoon vanilla

Powdered sugar

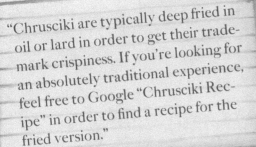

Ideas for Continued Learning

Explore: Poland shares its border with seven other countries. Consult a map and name the countries that share a border with Poland.

Learn: Marie Sklodowska (Also known as Marie Curie) was a famous Polish scientist. Research her name and learn what discoveries she is famous for.

POLAND

Capital City /	Warsaw
Nation Language /	Polish
Population /	38,383,809
Currency /	Złoty (PLN)

Poland *derived its name from the Slavic tribe that once lived in the flatlands of western Poland. The tribe's name, Polonia, translates as "the people living in the fields."*

The Legend of Baba Yaga

Baba Yaga is a complicated character; a twisted old witch who lives deep in the heart of the forest of Poland. Throughout history she's been depicted as living in a rambling old shack that hops around on chicken legs. Sometimes her house spins in circles to keep visitors from finding the front door, a spooky surprise for newcomers.

If Baba Yaga is having a bad day and doesn't want to talk to you, she'll fly away in her magical mortar and pestle, disappearing deep into the forest with no hopes of finding her again. In other words, you'll be pretty lucky if you get any face-to-face time with the fickle old lady.

Baba Yaga has answers for even the most difficult of questions. Rumor has it she ages one year for every question she is asked, so you can imagine any reluctance she may have to meeting you. The rare and magical blue rose helps Baba Yaga turn back the hands of time, so don't worry, she'll be around for many years to come.

Take a word of advice: if you see Baba Yaga deep in the forest, run in the opposite direction and you'll live to see another day!

Rose - *Rosa hybrid "Applause"*

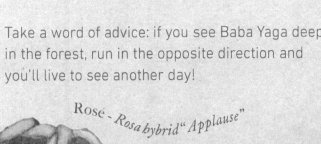

Getting to Know Poland

Fill in the missing information on this page. You can find the correct answers in your copy of *The Cultured Chef,* or search online to retrieve the information needed.

Capital City:

Country Population:

Language:

Google Poland's flag and use as reference to color the drawing below.

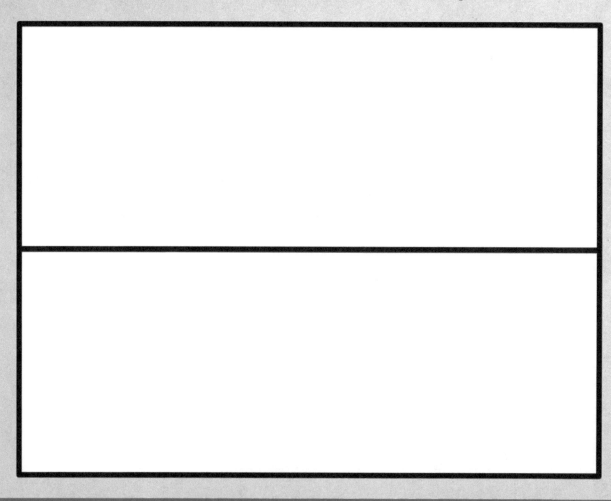

POLAND

A coat of arms is a design that various groups of people adopted in the middle ages to identify themselves in batte. The Polish coat of arms is based on the legend of Lech, one of the three brothers who founded the region. Lech claims to have seen a white eagle in a vision, with golden feathers colored by the setting sun. The vision inspired him, and the image now is represented in many Polish designs.

GETTING TO KNOW

Influential Europeans

Consider learning more about these important figures in European history. Their accomplishments have impacted the way of life not only for European citizens, but the world at large. When reviewing each of these accomplished individuals, please make note of the impact they made on society. Take a moment to reflect upon how your life is improved because of the achievements they made.

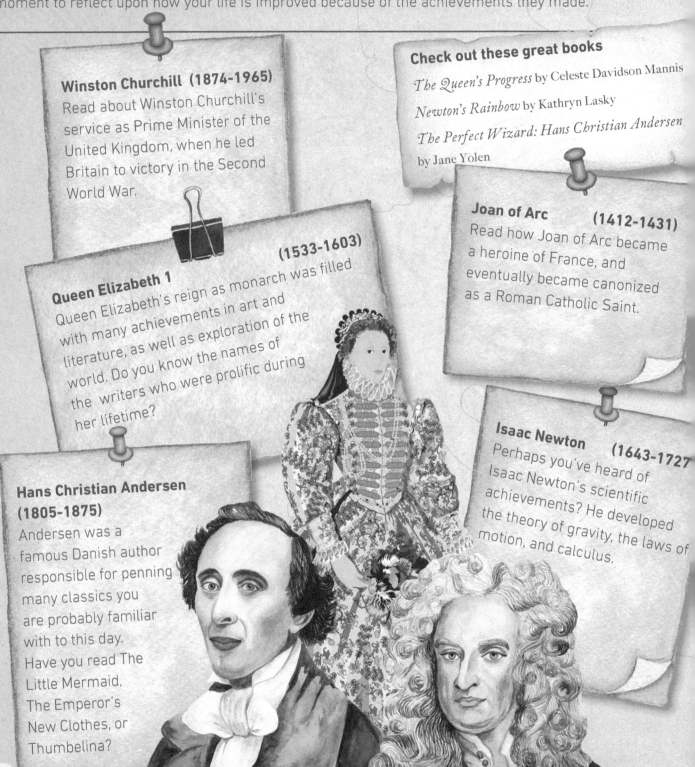

Winston Churchill (1874-1965)
Read about Winston Churchill's service as Prime Minister of the United Kingdom, when he led Britain to victory in the Second World War.

Check out these great books
The Queen's Progress by Celeste Davidson Mannis

Newton's Rainbow by Kathryn Lasky

The Perfect Wizard: Hans Christian Andersen by Jane Yolen

Queen Elizabeth 1 (1533-1603)
Queen Elizabeth's reign as monarch was filled with many achievements in art and literature, as well as exploration of the world. Do you know the names of the writers who were prolific during her lifetime?

Joan of Arc (1412-1431)
Read how Joan of Arc became a heroine of France, and eventually became canonized as a Roman Catholic Saint.

Isaac Newton (1643-1727)
Perhaps you've heard of Isaac Newton's scientific achievements? He developed the theory of gravity, the laws of motion, and calculus.

Hans Christian Andersen (1805-1875)
Andersen was a famous Danish author responsible for penning many classics you are probably familiar with to this day. Have you read The Little Mermaid, The Emperor's New Clothes, or Thumbelina?

Sweden

Swedish Pancakes (Pannkakor)

Did you know Swedish Pancakes have been prepared since the Middle Ages? That's a long history of deliciousness! Interestingly, Swedish Pancakes are rarely served for breakfast in Sweden. More often, they are enjoyed as a dessert with fresh fruit and whipped cream.

You can really show your creativity with this dish. Experiment with different fruit and berries if you like, and don't forget to be generous with the whipped cream!

Moose - *Alces alces*

The Great Grey Owl - *Strix nebulosa*

Swedish Pancakes (Pannkakor)

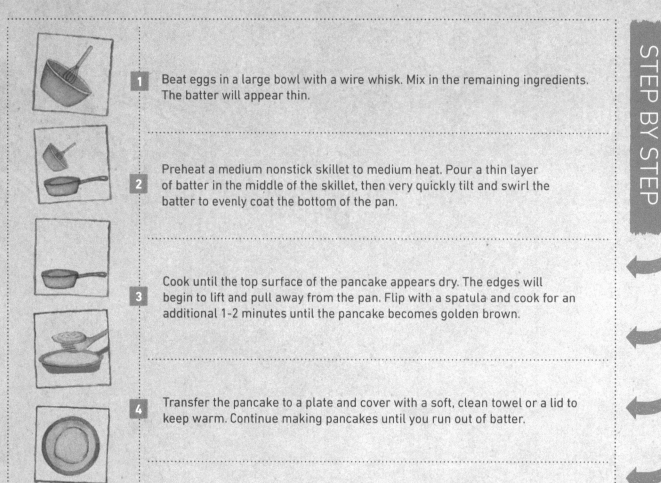

1. Beat eggs in a large bowl with a wire whisk. Mix in the remaining ingredients. The batter will appear thin.

2. Preheat a medium nonstick skillet to medium heat. Pour a thin layer of batter in the middle of the skillet, then very quickly tilt and swirl the batter to evenly coat the bottom of the pan.

3. Cook until the top surface of the pancake appears dry. The edges will begin to lift and pull away from the pan. Flip with a spatula and cook for an additional 1-2 minutes until the pancake becomes golden brown.

4. Transfer the pancake to a plate and cover with a soft, clean towel or a lid to keep warm. Continue making pancakes until you run out of batter.

A TIP JUST FOR KIDS!

You can serve Swedish Pancakes many different ways. Try them with berries and whipped cream, powdered sugar and lemon, or perhaps with a savory topping.

INGREDIENTS

4 eggs

2 cups milk

½ cup all-purpose flour

1 tablespoon sugar

1 pinch of salt

2 tablespoons butter, melted

Ideas for Continued Learning

Discover: The northern portion of Sweden is known as "The Land of the Midnight Sun" because during the summer months the sun never sets. Research this phenomenon and discuss with your friends.

Read: Read *Pippi Longstocking* by Swedish author, Astrid Lindgren.

SWEDEN

Capital City / Stockholm

Nation Language / Swedish

Population / 10,343,400

Currency / Swedish Krona

Take time to learn about famous artists and musicians from each country you study! Sweden is famous for being home to Astrid Lindgren (Creator of Pippi Longstocking) and the musical group ABBA. Filmmaker Ingmar Bergman, and actors Greta Garbo and Ingrid Bergman are also from Sweden.

Don't Mess with Trolls

The sun was sinking low in mid-winter sky, and Oscar's muscles had grown weary from cutting and splitting wood to sell in the village.

"You look like you could use a rest," wheezed a raspy voice from within the forest. Oscar dropped the handles of his wagon and whirled around, trying to determine where the voice was coming from. "I am here, young man.

Look into the forest," the voice called again. Oscar pushed aside branches as he made his way through the forest toward a high wall with a gate standing ajar. The closer he came to the gate, the more his senses became overwhelmed. He could feel the air grow warmer and sweeter. Beyond the open gate he could see a bountiful garden blooming with a colorful array of exotic flowers and luscious fruit.

"Rest your weary bones, then take some fruit home to your family," said the voice as he stepped into the pathway between Oscar and the garden. Oscar immediately recognized the speaker for what he was, a monstrous troll with jagged teeth, an oversized nose, and bushy grey hair that tumbled out from beneath the hood of his robe. The troll held out a giant red apple to tempt Oscar.

Oscar knew better than to trust a troll. He knocked the apple out of the troll's hand and ran through the forest back to his wagon. He could feel a source of heat growing stronger and stronger as he ran, and when he reached his wagon he turned around to see both the troll and the garden had erupted into flames, then quickly vanished into the night sky. Indeed, never trust a troll, as tempting as it may seem.

Getting to Know Sweden

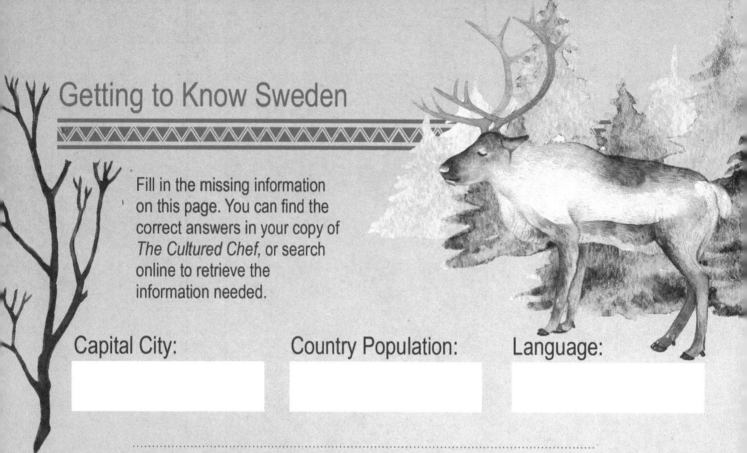

Fill in the missing information on this page. You can find the correct answers in your copy of *The Cultured Chef,* or search online to retrieve the information needed.

Capital City:

Country Population:

Language:

Google Sweden's flag and use as reference to color the drawing below.

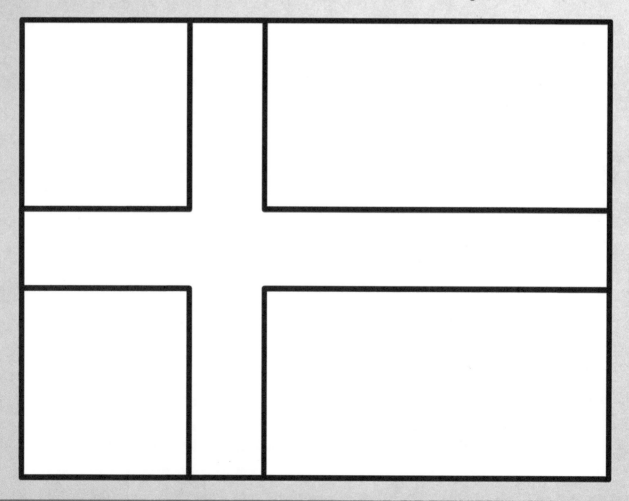

SWEDEN

Sweden - Pippi Longstocking

Pippi Longstocking is the beloved fictional character created by Swedish author Astrid Lindgren. The spunky character is known for her red hair and freckles. Pippi is featured in books, musicals, and television programs around the world. Have you read Pippi Longstocking?

LAVENDER OF PROVENCE

Citron Pressé

Most of Provence, a geographical region in southeastern France, has a Mediterranean climate with lots of sunshine. Aromatic plants such as sage, rosemary, wild thyme, and lavender thrive in this climate, so it makes sense the region has become a big producer of lavender commercially. One of the most beautiful sights you will ever witness is rolling hills of lavender on a bright and sunny day in Provence.

Here's a fun recipe for a refreshing drink almost everyone will love. Citron Pressé is a perfect treat for a hot, sunny day, and is enjoyed in cafes throughout the region of Provence.

In a small saucepan over medium heat, combine 1 cup of water with 1 cup of sugar, bring to a simmer and stir until the sugar is dissolved. Continue simmering for 5 minutes, be careful not to burn the mixture. Remove from the heat, add the lavender buds, stir well, and allow to steep for 20 minutes. After the mixture has cooled, use a fine mesh strainer to remove the bits of lavender. Discard the lavender and set aside the simple syrup mixture you have just prepared.

To prepare your drink, add some lemon juice to the bottom of a glass and add a spoonful of the simple syrup. Top with still or sparkling water, stir and taste. You can adjust the level of the lemon or sweetness as you desire. Add ice and a sprig of lavender for garnish. Enjoy!

INGREDIENTS

1 cup granulated sugar
Fresh-squeezed lemon juice
1 ½ teaspoons dried culinary
lavender buds
Chilled water (Sparkling is best)
Ice cubes
Sliced lemon for garnish

France

Croque Monsieur and Croque Madame

This tasty ham and cheese sandwich dates back to cafes in Paris in the early 1900s. The name in French is translated as "Mister Crunch." It's typically baked or fried in a skillet, and uses fine quality, thin slices of ham. Most recipes use a Béchamel sauce, an important sauce used in French cuisine made from butter, flour and milk. The only difference between a Croque Monsieur and Croque Madame is the latter has a fried egg on top.

Hydrangea - Hydrangea macrophylla

Croque Monsieur and Croque Madame

1 Make Your Sandwich: Spread mayonnaise on each slice of bread, then spread Dijon on the reverse side of each slice. On one slice of bread, layer the ham in-between the slices of cheese. Top with the other slice of bread, mustard-side down. (Make sure the mayonnaise sides face out.)

2 Fry Your Sandwich: Melt the butter in a large skillet over medium heat, then place the sandwich in the skillet to fry. Use a spatula to gently press the sandwich down while frying. Cook for several minutes, until the bread becomes golden brown. Flip the sandwich and repeat on the other side. Transfer to a plate.

A TIP JUST FOR KIDS!

If you'd like to turn your Monsieur into a Madame, fry an egg sunny side up and place it on top of the sandwich. Keep in mind, this is a simplified version of the sandwich. If you'd like to try a more complex version of the sandwich requiring Béchamel and baking, do an online search for recipes using that method.

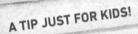

Ideas for Continued Learning

Celebrate: July 14th is Fête Nationale – Bastille Day, celebrated all over France. Discover for yourself what Bastille Day is all about.

Research: Notre-Dame de Paris is a world famous cathedral that was recently partially destroyed by fire. Find photos of this historic landmark before and after the fire.

INGREDIENTS

Makes one sandwich

2 slices white sandwich bread
2 tablespoons mayonnaise
1 tablespoon Dijon mustard
2-4 thin slices Gruyère cheese
1 1/2 tablespoons butter
1 tablespoons olive oil
1 large egg
Pinch of salt
Pinch of black pepper

FRANCE

Capital City / Paris	
Nation Language / French	
Population / 67,022,000	
Currency / Euro	

Chances are you've heard about the world famous Notre-Dame Cathedral in Paris, whether through literature (The Hunchback of Notre-Dame by Victor Hugo) or the 2019 fire that could have potentially destroyed the entire structure. Research the cathedral's history, and the current rebuilding efforts underway.

Jules Verne: One of the Fathers of Science Fiction

Jules Gabriel Verne (1828-1905) was a French novelist, poet and playwright who almost never reached his literary potential because of a career in law and finance. He initially followed in his father's footsteps as a lawyer, but quit so he could pursue writing instead. He's most famous for his adventure novels Journey to the Center of the Earth (1864), Twenty Thousand Leagues Under the Sea (1870), and Around the World in Eighty Days (1873).

Verne put a great deal of research into his books, exploring subjects he previously had no knowledge of. In fact, due to his research he was able to predict a number of advances in technology years ahead of their invention. He wrote about powered submarines, glass skyscrapers, calculators, high speed trains, as well as a worldwide communications network years before they were invented.

About the book Twenty Thousand Leagues Under the Sea: During the year 1866, ships of several nations spotted a mysterious sea monster. The United States government initiates an expedition to search for and destroy the monster.

About the book Around the World in Eighty Days: Phileas Fogg of London and his French valet attempt to travel around the world in 80 days, based on a bet made by his friends. They encounter many adventures.

Getting to Know France

Fill in the missing information on this page. You can find the correct answers in your copy of *The Cultured Chef*, or search online to retrieve the information needed.

Capital City:

Country Population:

Language:

Google France's flag and use as reference to color the drawing below.

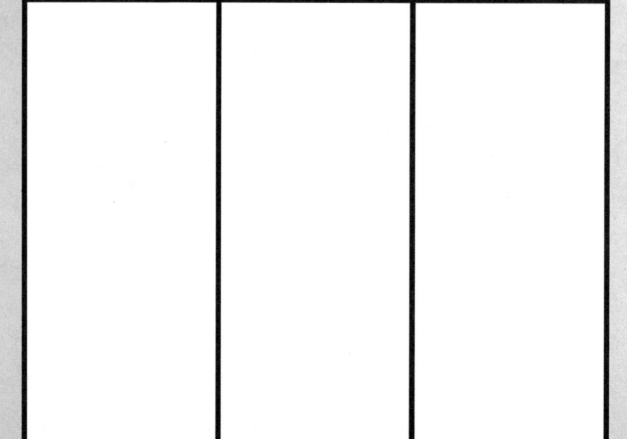

FRANCE

France - The Louvre Museum

The Louvre Museum (Musée du Louvre) is the largest art museum in the world, covering almost 800,000 square feet and hosting over 9 million visitors each year. Established more than 200 years ago, the museum's remarkable collection includes thousands of works of art.

Do you know the name of this famous painting by Leonardo da Vinci? You can view this priceless work of art when you visit the Louvre.

THE GUTENBERG PRESS

Germany is credited for producing one of the most important inventions in modern times. Johannes Gutenberg (1398-1468) was a German blacksmith, goldsmith and inventor credited with creating the moveable type printing press in the mid 1400's. Rather than using carved wooden blocks to press ink into paper, Gutenberg created moveable metal pieces to ink the pages.

Imagine the world without printed materials such as books, brochures, or any of the printed resources we use on a daily basis. In Gutenberg's day, it was very uncommon to have any kind of printed material in one's home. Gutenberg's press made such an impact, publishers could print thousands of pages in one day as opposed to the forty or fifty they could have produced before.

Gutenberg is most famous for printing and distributing one hundred and fifty to two hundred Bibles soon after the creation of his printing press. In those days, the Bibles sold for thirty florins, about three years wages for someone making a modest income. Today, twenty-one of the original Bibles remain intact, and could fetch as much as thirty million dollars at auction.

Johannes
Gutenberg

Germany

Potato Pancakes
(Kartoffelpuffer)

Potatoes were introduced in Germany in 1589 by a botanist who discovered them in Chile, and they have come to be an important part of German cuisine since that time. It's true, the average person in Germany eats between 130-140 lbs of potatoes each year. That's a whole lot of potatoes! They are served in soup, mashed, fried, and many other ways as well.

Potato pancakes are enjoyed throughout Germany with both sweet and savory toppings.

Potato Pancakes (Kartoffelpuffer)

1 Make sure the potatoes are as dry as possible. You can place them in cheesecloth or a clean towel to squeeze out any excess liquid, then pat dry.

2 Place the dried potato gratings in a medium-sized bowl with the onion, eggs, flour and salt. Use your hands to mix it all together. If the mixture appears too wet, you can add more flour so it becomes a nice tacky consistency. Don't let the mixture sit too long before frying.

3 Heat several tablespoons of oil in the bottom of a nonstick skillet on medium-high heat. Place ½ cup of the mixture in the plan and flatten into a pancake shape with a spatula. Fry the pancake on both sides for 3-5 minutes until it becomes a nice golden brown color. Pat them dry on paper towels when finished.

A TIP JUST FOR KIDS!

Potato pancakes are delicious when they are served hot with applesauce, preserves, fresh fruit, powdered sugar, sour cream, or anything else you think might taste good.

Ideas for Continued Learning

Celebrate: The winter markets in Germany are world famous due to the festive sights and sounds during the holiday season. Search Youtube for "German Christmas Markets" and see what you find.

Listen: Germany is famous for their many classical music composers. Listen to music by "Johann Sebastian Bach" and see if you recognize any of his work.

INGREDIENTS

2 1/2 pounds potatoes, peeled and very finely grated

1 small yellow onion, very finely grated

2 large eggs

1/4 cup all-purpose flour

1 teaspoon sea salt

Vegetable oil for frying

GERMANY

Capital City / Berlin

Nation Language / German

Population / 83,019,200

Currency / Euro

Germany is known for some of the most beautiful castles in the world, and you can see references to them throughout modern culture in art and literature. The Neuschwanstein Castle in Bavaria is considered to be the inspiration for Disney's Sleeping Beauty Castle. Did you know there are over 20,000 castles in Germany?

The Brothers Grimm

There's no doubt you've heard of some of the famous tales collected and rewritten by The Brothers Grimm. The brothers, Jacob Grimm (1785-1863) and Wilhelm Grimm (1786-1859), were German academics who worked as lawyers, librarians and eventually professors. They are most known for their collection of stories, Children's and Household Tales, first published in 1812.

They spent years collecting and rewriting many famous folktales that are well-known today because of their work. Cinderella, Hansel and Gretel, Rapunzel, Rumpelstiltskin, The Frog Prince, and even Snow White are among the tales they popularized.

What is a Folktale?

Folktales are stories that have been passed down from generation to generation. It is seldom that a folktale has a single author because each person who tells the story adds their own personal touches. Many folktales were centuries old, and made their way between different countries and even continents before anyone wrote them down. It is this reason the stories are called folktales because they are written by, and performed by "folk," or regular people.

Getting to Know Germany

Fill in the missing information on this page. You can find the correct answers in your copy of *The Cultured Chef*, or search online to retrieve the information needed.

Capital City:

Country Population:

Language:

Google Germany's flag and use as reference to color the drawing below.

Have you ever heard music featuring
the accordian? The accordian is a unique
instrument believed to have been invented
in Berlin, Germany. The instrument has become
popular all over the world, but it is featured prominently
in German folk music.

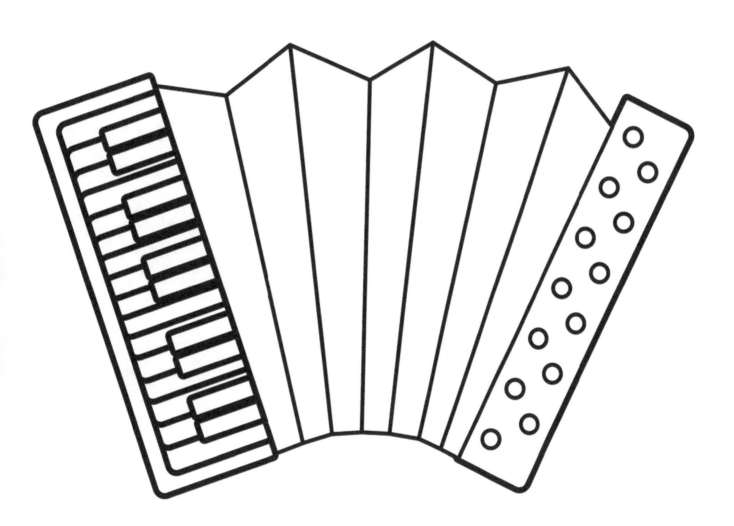

WORLD FESTIVALS & CELEBRATIONS

Discovering world festivals and celebrations becomes an important part of learning about other cultures. There is so much action, color and pageantry, it just makes you want to travel the world and experience it all! Check out these selections and see if you can find the additional world celebrations mentioned throughout the book. (Hint: Find Diwali, Dia de los Muertos, Carnival and more)

Mardi Gras - New Orleans

Mardi Gras, also known as Fat Tuesday, is an annual religious celebration that marks the last night of eating rich and fatty foods before a period of fasting. It's important to know there are many versions of this event that take place all over the world, but New Orleans Mardi Gras with its processions, costumes and masquerades has become world famous.

La Tomatina - Buñol, Spain

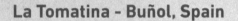

In late August each year, 20,000 people from all over the world buy tickets to experience the largest food fight on the planet. Large trucks carry one hundred and twenty tons of fresh tomatoes into the town square in Buñol, Spain, and for one hour attendees can throw tomatoes at one another until they become too exhausted to throw any more.

Lantern Festival - Pingxi, Taiwan

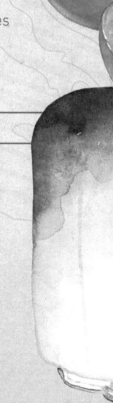

On the night of the first full moon of the lunar year, the people of Taiwan write messages and drawings representing their hopes and dreams all over paper lanterns. When the candle in the center of the lantern is lit, the flame heats the air inside the lantern and causes it to drift upward into the night sky. With paper lanterns of all shapes and sizes, the Lantern Festival is a sight to behold.

Portugal

Lemon Chicken Soup (Canja de Galinha)

Portuguese Lemon Chicken Soup is a traditional comfort food served in households all over Portugal. Chances are, if you were raised in a Portuguese family, your grandmother would make this soup for you if you weren't feeling well, or just needed some cheering up. Grandmothers are the best, aren't they?

Lemon Chicken Soup (Canja de Galinha)

1 Saute onions in olive oil until they start to become transparent. Add garlic and saute just a minute longer. Add in chicken stock (and a pinch of salt if the stock is homemade) Bring to a boil.

2 In a separate bowl, beat the egg yolks and lemon juice together until it forms a nice, golden sauce. Slowly mix in ¼ to ½ cup of the hot stock from the soup pot to keep the yolks from cooking too quickly, stirring gently.

3 Stir rapidly while adding the egg mixture to the hot soup. Taste the broth to determine if more salt is needed. Add the chicken and rice and cook on medium heat for 10-20 minutes. (Until the rice is thoroughly cooked) Add the chopped mint leaves.

A TIP JUST FOR KIDS!

This is one of my favorite recipes and I hope you enjoy it. You can replace the rice with bowtie pasta, elbow macaroni or orzo if you like. Just make sure you adjust the cooking time during step 3 until the noodle or rice of your choice is cooked thoroughly. Make this dish for someone you love when they aren't feeling well.

Ideas for Continued Learning

Draw: Portugal is famous for its painted tiles. Do a Google image search of "Azulejo tiles" and find your favorite design. See if you can draw it yourself!

Research: Look up photos of the beautiful cultural site "Bom Jesus do Monte, Braga."

INGREDIENTS

6 cups chicken stock

1 chicken breast, chopped or shredded

2 carrots, chopped

1 medium onion, diced small

2 cloves of garlic, minced (or pressed)

3 egg yolks, beaten

1 lemon, juiced

3 Tbs. mint leaves, chopped

1 cup Basmati rice

Salt to taste

PORTUGAL

Capital City / Lisbon

Nation Language / Portuguese

Population / 10,276,617

Currency / Euro

The Portuguese were major travelers and explorers throughout world history. In fact, they are largely responsible for sharing regional recipes and ingredients between countries long before cookbooks were published. Portuguese explorers and traders brought chili peppers, tomatoes and potatoes to India, ingredients that would later become a key component of Indian Cuisine.

The Story of Portugal's Barcelos Rooster

Sometimes miracles happen in the most unexpected ways. That's certainly true when it comes to the story of the Barcelos Rooster, a remarkable event that saved a man's life and has been remembered and shared for centuries.

Many years ago, a pilgrim and his teenage son were passing through the city of Barcelos. It was humid summer afternoon and they were very tired from walking for many hours. They stopped to rest on the steps of a grand estate, fanning themselves in the hot sun. The landowner spotted them and took pity, inviting them to join the festival taking place on his estate.

There was much delicious food and wine, and the father and son couldn't believe their luck. They ate and drank, then rested so they could continue their journey the next day. However, just as their eyes were about to close, a great ruckus erupted! "Thief! Thief! I invite these pilgrims into my home and one of them steals from me." The landowner accused the teenage pilgrim of stealing his precious silver.

"It's not true," said the boy's father. "I promise you he has nothing to do with your silver disappearing," he pleaded for the boy's innocence. He pointed to the dinner table where guests were still enjoying their food. "If my son is innocent, that roasted rooster on your plate will stand up and crow!"

Amused, the landowner and his guests erupted into laughter. But much to their immediate surprise, the cooked rooster stood up, walked to the edge of the table and let out a great, "Cock-a-doodle-do!" The boy's innocence was guaranteed, and the people of Barcelos remember this miraculous event to this day.

Getting to Know Portugal

Fill in the missing information on this page. You can find the correct answers in your copy of *The Cultured Chef,* or search online to retrieve the information needed.

Capital City:

Country Population:

Language:

Google Portugal's flag and use as reference to color the drawing below.

PORTUGAL

During the 15th and 16th centuries the Portuguese embarked upon extensive exploration by sea, creating some of the earliest known maps of the African, Asian Canadian and South American coastlines.

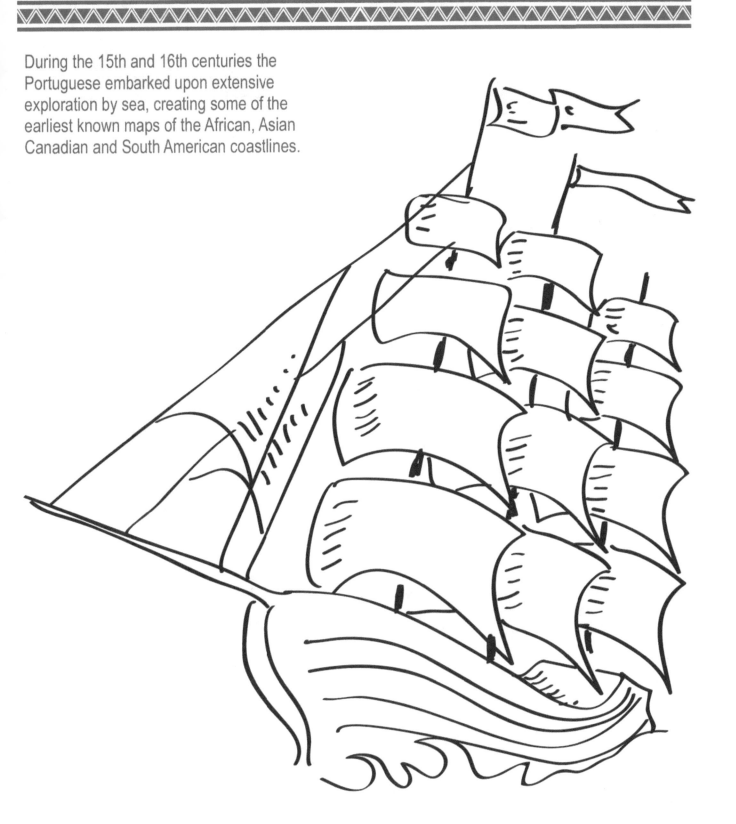

ACTIVITIES FOR THE KITCHEN

What Are Chopsticks Used For?

Research how people around the world eat their food. You can introduce new and fun ideas to your family and begin practicing dining customs from around the world. For example, when you cook and eat Asian food, use chopsticks. When eating foods from some African cultures, you are even supposed to eat with your hands! Visit your local library and talk with the librarians there about how to find books about different cultures.

How Much Does it Weigh?

Get your hands on a food scale whether you buy one or borrow one. Spend some time weighing different food items from your kitchen. Weigh several different kinds of foods in the same measuring cup and notice how much difference in weight there can be. For example, two cups of dry cereal will not weigh the same as two cups of flour.

How Much Will it Cost?

Go shopping—even if you have all the ingredients for your recipe. You do not have to buy anything. Just pay attention to how much the items cost and the total weight or amount. Then work out how much the amount of each ingredient will cost for your recipe. For example, say Greek yogurt is $5.27 for a quart-sized container and you want to figure out how much it will cost for the 2 cups you need to make Tzatziki Rolls on page 57-58 in the Greece section of this book.

First, check your measurement conversion chart. Two cups equals one pint. Two pints equals one quart. So, in this case you will need 1/2 of the total amount in the container for your recipe. Second, do the math:

Since you only need ½ of the container, you will divide the total cost by 2.

$5.27 / 2 = $2.635

Remember to round up to the nearest penny, making your cost for the yogurt in this recipe $2.64.

You can do this for all the ingredients in all your recipes. This is a fun way to practice some basic math skills for a real life purpose!

Hungary

Cheese Spread
(Körözött)

This Hungarian Cheese Spread is a favorite dish in many households throughout Hungary, and you will find many variations in how it is prepared. The most common attributes are caraway seeds that provide a unique flavor, and paprika for the color it provides. You can use this dish as a dip, or a spread for crackers and bread.

Cheese Spread (Körözött)

1 Mix all ingredients together until the mixture becomes a nice, creamy and consistent texture.

2 Let the mixture chill for 3 to 4 hour so the flavor is enhanced.

3 Spread the Körözött on bread or crackers, spread on top of sliced tomatoes, or served as a side with hard-boiled eggs. Use your imagination and enjoy.

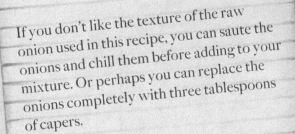

A TIP JUST FOR KIDS!

If you don't like the texture of the raw onion used in this recipe, you can saute the onions and chill them before adding to your mixture. Or perhaps you can replace the onions completely with three tablespoons of capers.

Ideas for Continued Learning

Experience: Have you played with a Rubik's Cube? It was invented by Ernő Rubik in Hungary!

Listen: Experience the Hungarian language by watching "Basic Hungarian Phrases" on Youtube.

INGREDIENTS

1 cup of cottage cheese

½ of a medium yellow onion – finely diced

½ stick of salted butter

¼ teaspoon dry mustard

1 teaspoon of sweet red paprika powder

1 level teaspoon of ground caraway seeds

1 tablespoon of sour cream

Salt to taste

HUNGARY

Capital City / Budapest	
Nation Language / Hungarian	
Population / 9,772,756	
Currency / Hungarian Forint	

You might be surprised to learn that parents can't name their child anything they like in Hungary. The name they choose has to come from a list of names approved by the government. While this may seem strange, it's true that many nations have rules about naming their children. In Hungary, Hunor and Hunyad are accepted names for boys, but if you want to name your child Hunter you're out of luck!

The Hedgehog's Journey

One day, the king and his men were hunting stags in the Gemenc forest when they became lost. They walked in circles for many hours until the afternoon sky began to darken. Soon the light would be gone, it would become very cold, and they'd be in danger of meeting with a hungry boar. The king said,"If only someone could help us find out way out of the forest, I would reward them with the hand of one of my three daughters, and three wagons full of gold and jewels!"

At that very moment, a hedgehog riding a cockerel (rooster) strode up beside the king. "I can help you, your majesty. And I will take the hand of your daughter and three wagons full of gold in return." The king laughed at the sight of a hedgehog riding a cockerel, but he was a man of his word. So he followed the hedgehog out of the forest and led him to his castle where he would claim his prize.

Upon hearing the news of their father's arrangement, the king's daughters lined up in front of the hedgehog. The first young woman burst into a fitful rage. "I will not marry this beast of the forest!' she said as she ran from the room.

The second daughter wept a great many tears, lamenting her uncertain future. The third daughter smiled and said, "I owe a great debt to the hedgehog who saved my father. I will gladly marry you." The king loaded the wagons full of gold, and sent his daughter and the hedgehog on their way. The young woman rode in the carriage, and the hedgehog on his cockerel.

After some time, the young woman inquired, "Dear husband, won't you ride with me in the carriage?" The hedgehog was surprised, "Aren't you sickened by the sight of your beastly husband?" She smiled, "Of course not, I love you very much!" With those words, the hedgehog turned into a handsome prince, the cockerel turned into a grand stallion, and they lived happily ever after.

Getting to Know Hungary

Fill in the missing information on this page. You can find the correct answers in your copy of *The Cultured Chef*, or search online to retrieve the information needed.

Capital City:

Country Population:

Language:

Google Hungary's flag and use as reference to color the drawing below.

Hungary - Széchenyi Chain Bridge

The Széchenyi Chain Bridge is the first permanent bridge crossing the Danube River between Buda and Pest, the western and eastern sections of the city of Budapest.

GARDEN TO TABLE

Garden Fresh Food

Consider growing some of the veggies that you would use in the recipes included in this book. In many cultures around the world, families rely on the vegetables they grow in their gardens to feed themselves. One of the ways you can differentiate different cultures around the world is by determining the kind of food they grow in their garden.

What people grow determines what they eat. What they grow depends on the soil, the climate, and the geographical area. For example, you are not going to be able to grow the same things in North Dakota that you would be able to grow in Southern Italy. Some plants need hotter weather and longer growing seasons. But no matter where you live or what you want to eat, homegrown vegetables can be far more delicious and much healthier than the ones you buy at the store.

You don't need a lot of space to grow vegetables. Even a five-foot square plot can yield a lot of food!. Check out these great books on gardening to see if this is something you'd like to try:

CHECK OUT THESE GREAT BOOKS ON GARDENING

- The Gardening Book by Jane Bull
- Family Garden by DK Publishing
- Kid's Container Gardening by Cindy Krezel

RUSSIA

Cold Beet Soup (Holodnik)

This cold beet soup is the summertime version of a very popular Eastern European soup called Borscht. The beets in the recipe give this dish the beautiful red color, while the egg and cucumber provide an interesting balance of flavor. I probably shouldn't say this, but growing up I couldn't stand eating Borscht when my mother prepared it. It wasn't until I became an adult that I realized I love beets. If you are adamantly opposed to beets, look to CulturedChef.com for alternative recipes.

A samovar is a device traditionally used to heat and boil water.

Cold Beet Soup (Holodnik)

1 Boil the beets, drain, and let them cool.

2 Boil 2 quarts of water and let it cool. Mix cooled water with 1 quart of buttermilk in a large pot.

3 Finely shred the beets with a grater or mandolin, then add them to the water/buttermilk mixture.

4 Add salt and sugar to taste. You may want more or less than the recipe calls for.

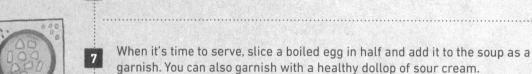

5 Next add chopped green onions, dill and diced cucumbers.

6 Place the combined ingredients in the refrigerator and let them completely chill.

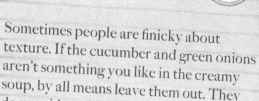

7 When it's time to serve, slice a boiled egg in half and add it to the soup as a garnish. You can also garnish with a healthy dollop of sour cream.

A TIP JUST FOR KIDS!

Sometimes people are finicky about texture. If the cucumber and green onions aren't something you like in the creamy soup, by all means leave them out. They do provide a nice balance of flavor, and a little crunch as well.

Ideas for Continued Learning

Watch: Search for "Prisyadka" or Russian Squat Dance on Youtube. This traditional dance is very energetic and fun to watch!

Research: Russia has some of the most beautiful architecture in the whole world. Search "Russian Architecture" in Google and see the variety of buildings.

INGREDIENTS

3 large cooked red beets (5 small)

2 quarts boiled cooled water

1 quart buttermilk

1 bunch green onions, finely chopped

4 cucumbers, diced

1 tablespoon sea salt

1 teaspoon sugar

1 bunch dill, finely chopped

4-6 boiled eggs

RUSSIA

Capital City /	Moscow
Nation Language /	Russian
Population /	146,793,744
Currency /	Russian Ruble

In terms of land area, Russia is the biggest country in the world. It shares its border with fourteen countries and occupies one-tenth of all the land on Earth! It's hard to imagine the vastness of such a large country, but consider this: Russia touches the shores of three oceans (Atlantic, Pacific and Arctic) and stretches across eleven time zones!

Legend of the Matryoshka

Nesting dolls are wooden dolls that decrease in size and are placed inside one another - as many as five to ten dolls sometimes. Matryoshka Dolls were created in the late 1800's by the Children's Education Workshop, a group of Russian woodworkers and artists. The dolls have become closely associated with Russian culture, but it should be noted that the concept of nesting boxes and dolls date back many hundreds of years to China and Japan.

The sunshine peeked through the dusty window as little, old grandmother and her family worked to make brightly colored scarves for the upcoming community festival. Young Oksana couldn't wait to dance with her scarf flowing in the breeze, so she twirled around and around practicing her graceful moves.

Grandma cried out, "Oksana, you are distracting us from our work. Please go dance outside if you are not going to help!" Oksana didn't say a word, she twirled around and around as she passed through the door into the garden. She twirled down the path to the community trail, and beyond that into the valley below.

Soon, one of Oksana's sisters cried, "Grandmother, look! Oksana is in danger, she has danced too far!" Grandmother dropped her scarf and rushed out the door to protect her youngest granddaughter.

Grandmother cried, "Oksana, come back! You've strayed too far." She was followed by her daughter, Oksana's mother, who cried, "My daughter, please stop dancing!" Mother was followed by her eldest daughter, who also yelled for Oksana to stop dancing.

The neighboring farmers watched as one by one, the sisters reached Oksana and scooped her into their arms. Mother and Grandmother arrived last, being older and slower, until the entire family was wrapped in a warm embrace.

FUN FACTS

Matryoshka means "little matron," or head of the family. The world record for the largest set of Matryoshka dolls was created in 2003 by Russian artist Youlia Bereznitskaia. There are 51 dolls in the set. The largest stands over 11 feet tall, and the smallest is just 0.12.

Getting to Know Russia

Fill in the missing information on this page. You can find the correct answers in your copy of *The Cultured Chef,* or search online to retrieve the information needed.

Capital City:

Country Population:

Language:

....

Google Russia's flag and use as reference to color the drawing below.

RUSSIA

Russia -

St Basil's Cathedral in the
Red Square of Moscow is
considered one of the most
iconic landmarks in Russia.
Google this church to see
the colorful domes.

The Flora and Fauna of Europe

Europe is the sixth largest continent in size and third largest when population is considered. It is bordered by the Mediterranean Sea, Asia, and the Atlantic Ocean. Those studying flora and fauna of Europe will find many of the large animals and top predator species have been hunted to extinction. Review the chart below and discover your favorite animals.

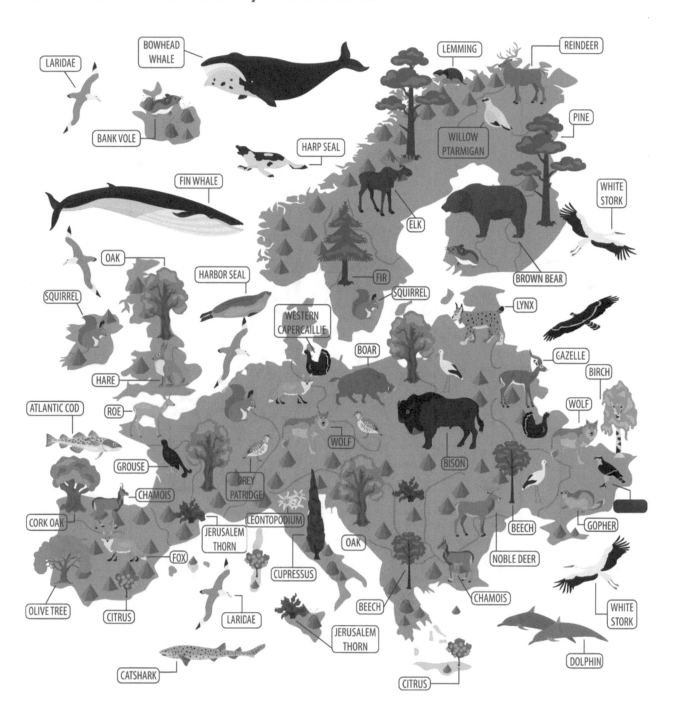

Animals
of Europe

There is a lot to consider when learning about animals of the world. Different animals are suited to different climates, and have particular tastes when it comes to the food they need to survive. A penguin won't feel very much at home on the beach in Miami, Florida, would it?

Select an animal from the previous page about Europe and write a short report below. Where does the animal live? What does the animal like to eat? Are there any other facts about this animal you find interesting?

Use the space below to write down interesting facts about the animal you have chosen.

ASIA

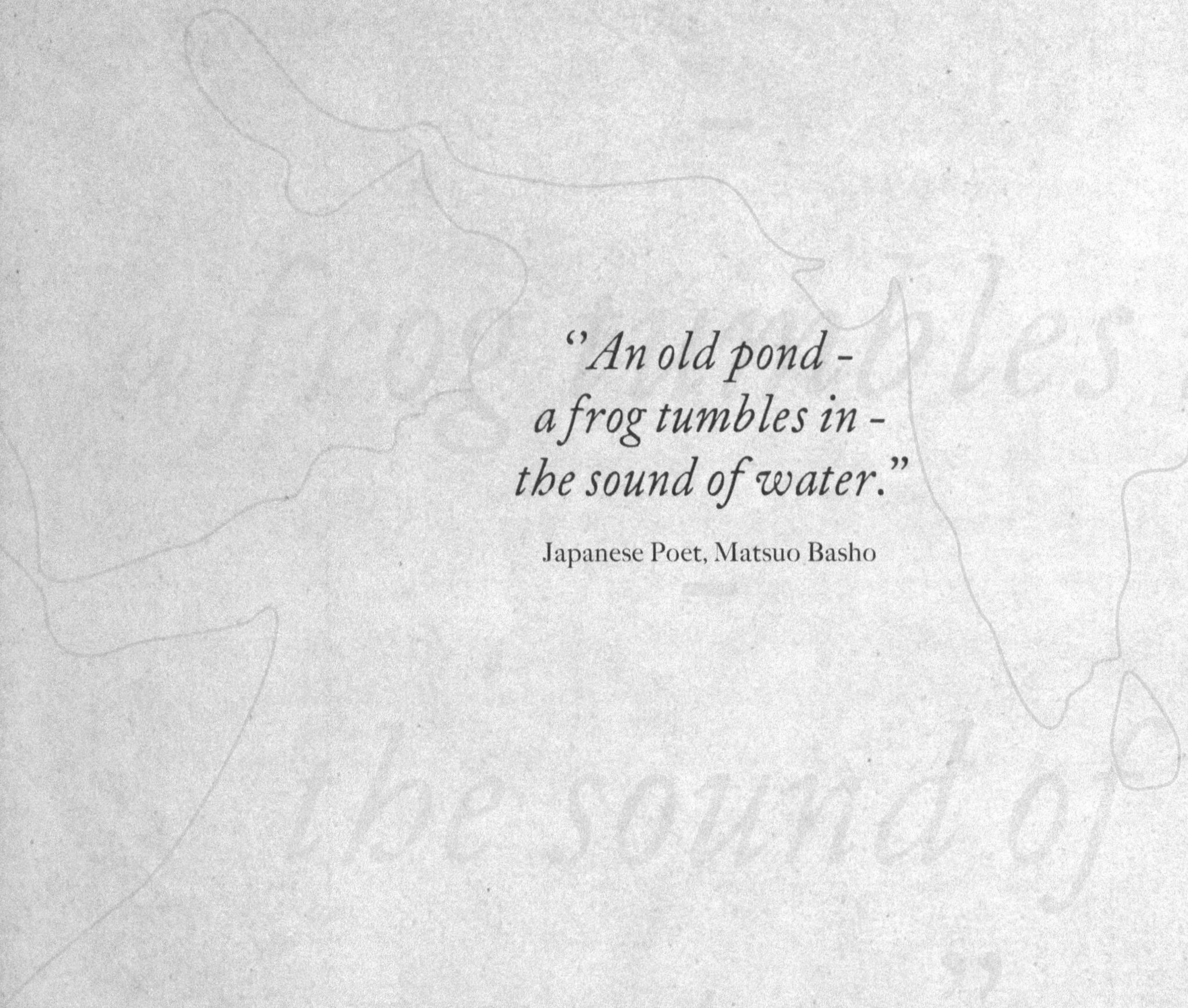

"*An old pond -
a frog tumbles in -
the sound of water.*"

Japanese Poet, Matsuo Basho

ASIA

INDIA - THAILAND - CHINA - MYANMAR - JAPAN - REPUBLIC OF KOREA - IRAN

INDIA

Om: *(the symbol of Hinduism) The sound "Om" represents energy in its simplest form, describing the essence of everything that is pure and natural.*

A Rich and Diverse Culture

With a population of more than 1.2 billion people, and a recorded history dating back many thousands of years, it is impossible to describe the complex diversity of Indian culture in a paragraph or two. India's unique languages, religions, music, food, architecture and mythology differ from place to place within the country.

Indian history and culture is full of many interesting gods, goddesses and mythical beings that are fun to explore in more depth. Perhaps visit your local librarian and ask for assistance in researching Indian culture and folk tales. There is much to discover.

Saraswati is the goddess of knowledge, music and the arts.

Diwali is known as the Hindu Festival of Lights, an event where thousands of small, decorative lamps are lit representing the triumph of good over evil.

Lakshmi is the goddess of wealth and prosperity.

Ganesha is the god of intellect and the remover of obstacles.

Mahatma Gandhi *said, "If we could change ourselves, the tendencies in the world would also change." He was one of the most important leaders in the fight for independence from England, well-known for his belief in non-violent activism.*

Cucumber and Lime Salad
(Khamang Kakdi)

Khamang Kakdi is a traditional recipe originating from the Maharashtra region in western India. Although ancient poems indicate the Maharashtra region was once only inhabited by exiled criminals and holy men, it is now the second largest state in India. What a difference 3,000 years can make!

The Maharashtrians (or Marathi people) observe a number of holy days that require many to not eat any food (fasting) for a period of time. Fasting can be difficult for some people, so there are a handful of food items the Marathi can eat, including this cucumber and lime salad.

163

Cucumber and Lime Salad (Khamang Kakdi)

1 In a large bowl, place cucumber, peanuts, two tablespoons of coconut, lime juice and agave syrup together.

2 In a small sauté pan, heat the oil. Add mustard seeds, stirring them until they start to crackle and pop. At this point add the cumin, salt and remaining coconut and continue stirring until the ingredients are evenly mixed. Turn off the heat.

3 Pour the sauté pan contents over the cucumber mixture, add cilantro and mix until the cucumbers are evenly coated. Season with salt or additional agave syrup until the mixture has your desired salty-sweet ratio.

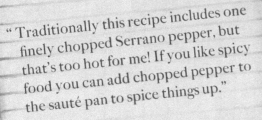

A TIP JUST FOR KIDS!

" Traditionally this recipe includes one finely chopped Serrano pepper, but that's too hot for me! If you like spicy food you can add chopped pepper to the sauté pan to spice things up."

Ideas for Continued Learning

Watch: Have you experienced the magic of a Bollywood Musical? You can find these films on Youtube, as well as Netflix. Watch a clip (or an entire film) and discuss with your family.

Research: Do a Google image search for "Indian Fashion" and discuss the colorful costumes with a friend.

INGREDIENTS

1 English cucumber, cubed, 3-4 cups

2/3 cup shelled peanuts, finely chopped

1/2 cup unsweetened coconut, shredded

2 tablespoons fresh lime juice

1/2 teaspoon agave syrup

2 tablespoons olive oil

1/2 cup cilantro, finely chopped

1/2 teaspoon brown mustard seeds

1/2 teaspoon cumin

1/2 teaspoon salt

1/2 teaspoon cayenne pepper

INDIA

Capital City / New Delhi	
Nation Language / Hindi /English / others	
Population / 1,210,193,422	
Currency / India Rupee	

India *is one of the most populated countries in the world, second only to China, with over 1.2 billion people calling it home. It is projected India's population will surpass China's before the year 2030, when it is expected to reach 1.6 billion people.*

Mehndi: An Indian Wedding Tradition

Lawsonia inermis - Commonly known as Henna, this flowering plant is prized for the dye made from its crushed and powdered leaves. Used worldwide for cosmetic purposes such as dying hair and fabric, it is mostly used for making henna tattoos, known as Mehndi.

According to Hindu tradition, both men and women have been using henna to create ceremonial tattoos since ancient times in India. Typically the mehndi ceremony takes place several days before a marriage ceremony. The event is a festive celebration with women wearing bright, colorful dresses and performing traditional dances. There is lively music and lots of food for everyone.

The henna paste is applied to the hands and feet forming intricate patterns that include important Hindu symbolism as well as the names of the bride and groom. It can take many hours for a mehndi design to be applied, but when complete it can last for several weeks. In fact, tradition states the longer a mehndi design lasts, the longer the new wife can refrain from doing housework.

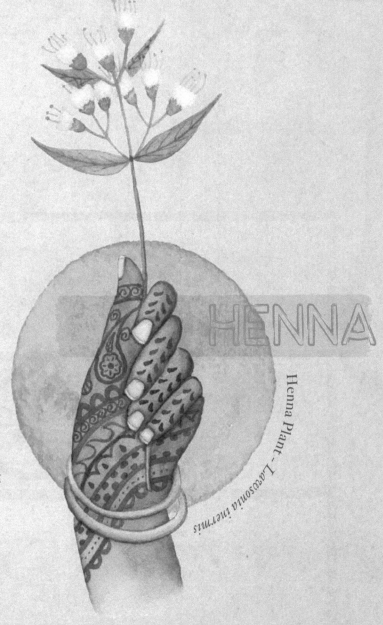

HENNA

Henna Plant - *Lacosonia inermis*

Getting to Know India

Fill in the missing information on this page. You can find the correct answers in your copy of *The Cultured Chef,* or search online to retrieve the information needed.

Capital City:

Country Population:

Language:

Google India's flag and use as reference to color the drawing below.

INDIA

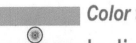
Elephants are considered
sacred in Indian culture as
they represent power, dignity,
intelligence and peace. The
Hindu god Ganesha is depicted
as having the head of an elephant.

Thailand

Buddha

Many years ago in 580 BC, Siddhārtha Gautama was born into a royal family and spent his childhood living behind the protection of palace walls. He was sheltered from the hunger and poverty of the surrounding villages.

It was only when Siddhārtha was married with a child that he first witnessed the problems outside the palace walls. These problems convinced him to leave the safety of his palace to discover whether life could be lived without suffering. He spent years traveling as a wandering monk and learned that sickness, aging and death were inescapable — a fate no one could avoid.

His travels failed to answer Siddhārtha's questions, so he began to look inward. Through meditation, he found a state of mind that was free from suffering called Nirvana. At the age of 35, he became known as Buddha, the Supreme Enlightened One.

Sacred Lotus - Nelumbo nucifera

Buddha

Siddhartha Gautama

Mango Sticky Rice

(Khao Niaow Ma Muang)

Prepared in kitchens all over Thailand, Mango Sticky Rice is a popular dessert made of rice, sweetened coconut milk and mangoes. Delicious and traditional, this dish is easy to prepare. The most important ingredient is the mangoes, of course. But don't worry if you don't have mangoes in your kitchen. You can prepare this recipe with any other sweet fruit, including peach, papaya, banana, cantaloupe or apricot.

Durian – Durio kutejensis

The Spirit House *is a shrine dedicated to the spirits in charge of protecting specific homes or locations in Southeast Asian countries. Spirits can be tricky if they're not happy, so the spirit house provides a place to present offerings.*

Buddhism *is the name of the religion formed by people who choose to live as the Buddha did. These followers try not to do anything bad, to do good deeds and to purify their minds through meditation. Buddhism is practiced all over the world and is the primary religion of Thailand.*

Mango Sticky Rice

1 Prepare rice as directed on packaging.

2 While the rice is cooking, heat the coconut milk until hot; avoid boiling. Stir in sugar and salt until completely dissolved.

3 Place prepared rice in a medium-size mixing bowl and pour half the coconut milk over, saving the rest for later. Evenly distribute the coconut milk through the rice and allow the flavors to blend.

4 Peel the mangoes. (See mango peeling instructions.)

5 Arrange a small mound of sticky rice on individual dessert plates and display the cut mangoes decoratively on top or to the side of the rice. Top with the extra coconut milk mixture.

A TIP JUST FOR KIDS!

How to Peel a mango:
With the stem pointing down, cut the mango into three strips from top to bottom. (two outer sides and a smaller mid-section containing the pit) Next, take each of the strips and cut lengthwise and crosswise, forming little cubes. Use a spoon to remove the cubes, and discard the pit.

Ideas for Continued Learning

Explore: Let's have some fun. Plan an imaginary trip to Thailand. What cities would you like to visit and why? Pick two interesting things you'd like to see in each city.

Learn: The Thai alphabet (or Abugida) is very different than English. Do a Google image search for "Thai Script" and compare.

INGREDIENTS

3 cups sticky rice (also labeled "glutinous rice" or "sweet rice"), soaked overnight in water or thin coconut milk and drained

2 cups canned coconut milk

3/4 cup palm sugar, or substitute brown sugar

1 teaspoon salt

4 ripe mangoes, or substitute sliced ripe peaches or papayas

Mint or Asian basil sprig

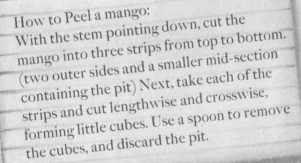

THAILAND

Capital City / Bangkok	
Nation Language / Thai	
Population / 66,720,153	
Currency / Thai baht	

Thailand is called Prathet Thai in the Thai language, which translates to "land of the free." The name makes sense when you consider Thailand is the only region in Southeast Asia that has escaped colonization by European countries.

The Exotic Fruit of Thailand

Purple Mangosteen: *Garcinia mangostana* - The fruit of the mangosteen is juicy and sweet with a bit of a tangy aftertaste. The outer purple-reddish rind is inedible, leaving only the inner white portion to enjoy. The fruit grows on a tree that is believed to have originated in the Sunda Islands of Indonesia.

Durian: *Durio kutejensis* - This massive fruit (12-15 inches long by 6 inches wide) is known as the "king of the fruits." People are strongly divided as to whether they like the fruit or not because of its pungent aroma. Some say it smells like raw sewage, others say rotting onions. Maybe you should be the judge?

Lychee: *Litchi chinensis* - Lychee is extremely popular in China, Southeast Asia and India where it is grown, as well as countries all over the world where it is exported. The outer portion of the fruit is covered with a bumpy red rind that is not edible. The pulpy flesh inside is fragrant and sweet.

Getting to Know Thailand

Fill in the missing information on this page. You can find the correct answers in your copy of *The Cultured Chef,* or search online to retrieve the information needed.

Capital City:

Country Population:

Language:

Google Thailand's flag and use as reference to color the drawing below.

THAILAND

The Garuda is a mythological
birdlike creature that appears
in Buddhist and Hindu myths.

Learn a Foreign Language

Learning a foreign language helps us to better communicate with our friends and neighbors. High schools in the United States require students to study a foreign language, but many students don't enjoy the experience. What about you? Why not try to make learning a foreign language fun? Many phrasebooks, games and apps are available to make learning a new language fun.

Use Google Translate to Translate These Phrases

Spanish: ¿Tienes hermanos o hermanas?

French: Comment allez-vous?

French: Pouvez-vous m'aider?

German: Können Sie das übersetzen?

German: Ich brauche Auskunft.

Italian: Mi scusi, quanto costa?

Hawaiian: Hau'oli Makahiki Hou!

Dutch: Een prettige dag gewenst.

CHINA

Tea Leaf Eggs

These boiled eggs with a marbled pattern are a traditional treat for the Chinese New Year, but you can also find them sold in stores, restaurants and from street vendors throughout mainland China. The eggs represent fertility and prosperity, and they make the house smell amazing while they are being prepared.

This is a very fun activity to share as a family. The patterns that unfold as you are removing the shell from the egg are remarkable. And no two eggs are alike!

Koi - Cyprinus rubrofuscus

Tea Leaf Eggs

1 Place the eggs in a medium saucepan, making sure they are completely submerged with at least 1 inch of water over the top of the eggs. Bring the water to a boil, then lower the heat to simmer for 20 minutes.

2 Remove the eggs from the hot water (save the water) and place in a bowl of cold water to cool.

3 When the eggs have cooled completely, gently tap the shell with a teaspoon all over the egg. Try to prevent any large chunks falling off, as the goal is to only create a spiderweb of cracks all over the egg. Set the eggs aside when complete.

4 Add all of the remaining ingredients to the egg water. Gently return the eggs to the water and bring to a low boil; then lower the heat to simmer.

5 Let the eggs simmer for two hours, but make sure the water stays high enough to cover the eggs. After two hours, turn off the heat and let the eggs soak in the tea water for an additional 2-3 hours. The longer the eggs soak, the deeper the color will be. Remove the shells to serve.

A TIP JUST FOR KIDS!

I am a big fan of listening to traditional music while preparing authentic food. Search Youtube for the ancient Chinese melody called Yangguan Sandie. Listen to several versions of this song as it can be performed on a variety of traditional instruments.

Ideas for Continued Learning

Explore: The Chinese garden is an art that is celebrated around the world. Perhaps you have a Chinese garden in your community. Plan a visit when you can.

Research: Do a Google Image Search for "The Great Wall of China." Perhaps you can trace this wall on a map, or watch a Youtube video on the history of this landmark.

INGREDIENTS

8 large eggs
3 ½ cups water
2 tablespoons loose black tea
2 Star anise, crushed
1 3-inch cinnamon stick
1 teaspoon brown sugar
1 tablespoons soy sauce
1 teaspoon fennel
1 teaspoon cloves
1 teaspoon black peppercorns
½ teaspoon dried orange peel

CHINA

Capital City / Beijing

Nation Language / Mandarin / Cantonese

Population / 1,403,500,365

Currency / Renminbi (Yuan)

It's amazing to consider all of the technical innovations made in Ancient China. For example, did you know paper was invented in China many, many years ago? The magnetic compass, silk, porcelain, printing and gunpowder were invented in China as well.

Chinese New Year: The Legend of Monster Nian

In the ancient days of China, when tiny villages were networked by dusty trails all across the land, there lived a big-horned, lion-headed monster named Nian. The monster lived at the bottom of the sea, and emerged once a year to strike fear in the hearts of all who encountered it. The monster would flash it's long, sharp teeth, devour livestock, and chase the terrified villagers out of their homes.

An old man happened upon the village one year, just as everyone was preparing to escape to the mountains. "Run for safety, the monster is coming," shouted the villagers as he sat motionless by the side of the road. "I will rid your village of the monster if you allow me a place to stay," he offered a woman who held her child tightly. "Do as you wish, but you are best to hide in the hills," she responded. The old man ignored her advice and made himself comfortable in her home.

Late that evening there was a wild rumpus in the village and the old man rushed to the street with a red lantern to light his way. As the monster rounded the corner and began charging at the courageous man, it stopped suddenly and howled a terrifying howl. The old man clanged a nearby bell and made as much noise as he could, hoping to frighten the monster even more. The monster bolted toward the sea, panicking and shrieking because of the unexpected surprise.

The villagers were amazed when they returned to the village. Their homes were still standing, their livestock were safe, and the courageous old man survived the night. He shared his secret with them. He discovered Nian is frightened of the color red, bright lights and loud noises. So from that day forward, the villagers would light firecrackers and place red decorations on their doors, thereby protecting themselves from the monster.

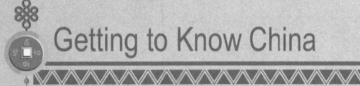

Getting to Know China

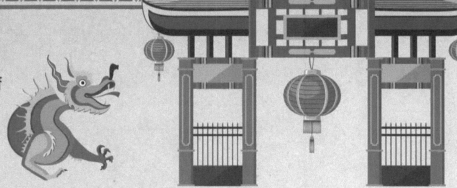

Fill in the missing information on this page. You can find the correct answers in your copy of *The Cultured Chef*, or search online to retrieve the information needed.

Capital City:

Country Population:

Language:

Google China's flag and use as reference to color the drawing below.

CHINA

Chinese culture has long looked to the dragon as a symbol of power, strength and good luck.

GETTING TO KNOW

Influential Asians

Consider learning more about these important figures in Asian history. Their accomplishments have impacted the way of life not only for citizens throughout Asia, but the world at large. When reviewing each of these accomplished individuals, please make note of the impact they made on society. Take a moment to reflect upon how your life is improved because of the achievements they made.

Matsuo Bashō   (1644-1694)
Matsuo Bashō was a Japanese poet, well known throughout the world for his haiku. Many monuments and public buildings throughout Japan carry inscriptions with his writings.

Check out these great books
Malala: My Story of Standing Up for Girls' I
by Sarah J. Robbins & Malala Yousafzai

I Am Gandhi   by Brad Meltzer

Basho and the River Stones   by Tim J. Myers

Mahatma Gandhi   (1869-1948)
Mahatma Gandhi was one of the most important leaders in the fight for India's independence from England. He is well-known for his beliefs in non-violent activism.

Confucius   (551-479 BCE)
Confucius was a Chinese politician, statesman, teacher and philosopher. He wrote extensively on issues related to justice, life and society.

Captain Prem Mathur (1910-1992)
Captain Prem Mathur became the first female pilot for a commercial Indian airline in 1947. She was rejected by eight other airlines before finding a job with Deccan Airlines.

Malala Yousafzai   (1997-)
Malala Yousafzai is a young Pakistani human rights activist specializing in the education of women and children in regions where resources are limited or denied. She was awarded the Nobel Peace Prize in 2014.

Myanmar

Myanmar Fried Rice

Out of respect, the oldest members of the families in Myanmar are always served their meals first. In fact, even if grandparents are missing at mealtime, the first grain of rice is scooped from the pot and set aside in their honor.

This rice dish is quick, healthy and delicious, and is a staple at tables throughout Myanmar. Here's an interesting fact - did you know that rice is eaten for breakfast, lunch, dinner and even dessert in other cultures? In one way or another, rice is a main ingredient for many dishes around the world.

Orchid - Orchidaceae

Did you know there are nearly 1000 varieties of orchids that grow naturally in Myanmar? The warm and humid climate allows the orchids to thrive.

Green Peafowl - Pavo muticus

181

Myanmar Fried Rice

1 Heat the oil in a skillet (or wok, if you have one) over medium-high heat. Add turmeric and let it dissolve in oil. Next, add the shallots and let cook for about 3 minutes until they start to become transparent, stirring frequently. Add the ginger and garlic and cook for an additional 45 seconds to 1 minute.

2 Add the rice and mix all the ingredients well. Add the peas, salt, and sliced scallions. Continue cooking the rice mixture until it has heated evenly.

3 Garnish the dish with cilantro or pepper flakes if you like a little spice. Serve as a single dish, or pair with another vegetable or meat dish.

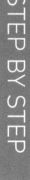

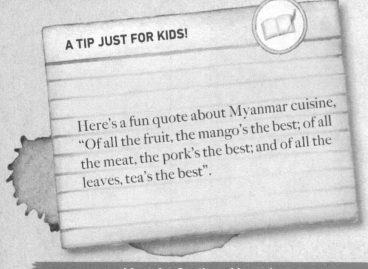

A TIP JUST FOR KIDS!

Here's a fun quote about Myanmar cuisine, "Of all the fruit, the mango's the best; of all the meat, the pork's the best; and of all the leaves, tea's the best".

Ideas for Continued Learning

Explore: Search for "Kyaiktiyo Pagoda" or Golden Rock for an unusual surprise. This site is one of Myanmar's most important pilgrimage sites.

Listen: Experience traditional music from Myanmar. Search Youtube for "Traditional Myanmar Music." How does it compare to music you hear at home?

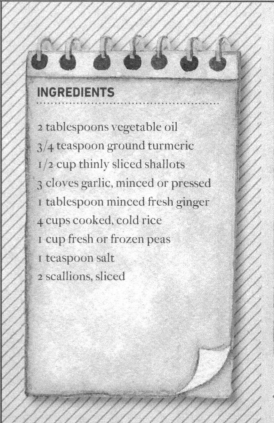

INGREDIENTS

2 tablespoons vegetable oil
3/4 teaspoon ground turmeric
1/2 cup thinly sliced shallots
3 cloves garlic, minced or pressed
1 tablespoon minced fresh ginger
4 cups cooked, cold rice
1 cup fresh or frozen peas
1 teaspoon salt
2 scallions, sliced

MYANMAR

Capital City /	Naypyidaw
Nation Language /	Burmese
Population /	53,582,855
Currency /	Kyat

Nearly half of Myanmar is covered with forests that are full of all sorts of interesting wild animals. Myanmar is home to elephants, rhinoceros, tigers, leopards, and water buffalo, as well as many unusual and exotic birds like parrots and peafowl.

The Old Man and the Prince

Mangoes have the honor of being one of the most widely consumed fruits in the world, and they hold a special place in Myanmar. The entire mango tree is very useful for the people of Myanmar. The fruit is edible when it is big or small, the leaves are nutritious and can be added to salads, and the wood is very strong and can be used to make furniture.

One day a little old man was working hard in the afternoon sun, planting mango trees along a path in the countryside. A young prince walked by and the old man offered him a ripe mango from one of the older trees nearby. "Your highness, would you like this fresh mango for your travels?"

"Grandpa, thank you very much for your kindness. I can see you are a good man. May I ask, how old are you?" The old man replied, "I am 88-years-old, but I have the energy of a young man."

"Yes, I can see this to be true," the prince smiled as he surveyed the progress the old man continued to make as he planted the trees. "Because you are a very old man, I don't believe you will ever enjoy the fruit from the trees you are planting. Can you tell me why you spend your time doing the work of a young man?"

The old man laughed, "The mango you are eating now, that tree was planted by my grandfather 70 years ago, and the fruit has been enjoyed by many." He motioned to the row of saplings he was planting along the trail and continued, "The fruit from the trees I am planting now will be enjoyed by my grandchildren, and their grandchildren many years from now."

"Thank you, wise Grandpa," said the prince. "I have learned a great lesson from you." Indeed, the prince grew to be a very generous king who provided well for his people. He never forgot the hard work and generosity of the little old man he met that day.

Getting to Know Myanmar

Fill in the missing information on this page. You can find the correct answers in your copy of *The Cultured Chef*, or search online to retrieve the information needed.

Capital City:

Country Population:

Language:

Google Myanmar's flag and use as reference to color the drawing below.

MYANMAR

Myanmar - Intha Fisherman of Inle Lake

The Intha fisherman on Inle Lake in Myanmar are famous for their unique method of fishing and navigating their boats on the lake. Look up Intha fishermen on Youtube to watch these fishermen at work.

THE WORLD OF TEA

It's easy to run to the grocery store to pick up a package of tea, but have you ever considered the complex history and traditions of tea around the world?

According to Chinese legend, Emperor Shennong was greatly pleased with the improved flavor of his water when a dried leaf from a plant fell into his cup. Whether this story is true or not, drinking tea is a custom that dates back many thousands of years. Tea is enjoyed for relaxation, health benefits, as well as dying fabric and paper!

Tea Bags: Tea has been packaged in paper packets for transport for many, many years, but it was only in the early 1900's that tea bags were packaged for the purpose of steeping in water. The earliest bags were small sacks made of fabric, but later paper, silk and synthetic fabrics became popular. Tea bags were packed by hand until 1929 when a machine was invented in Germany to make the process much easier.

England: Would you believe me if I told you taking tea is a relatively new custom in England? If you consider the nation's lengthy history, it's fascinating to realize afternoon tea was introduced in the mid-1800's. It became popular with the upper classes to have a light, late afternoon meal consisting of small sandwiches and cakes with tea. Note: Tea was introduced to England in the 17th century, but it took a while to catch on.

Japan: The preparation and serving of tea has been an important cultural tradition in Japan for many years. A traditional Japanese tea ceremony, known as The Way of Tea, requires a skilled server to prepare powdered green tea (matcha) with special tools in a tranquil setting. It takes many years to study tea ceremony and perfect the art.

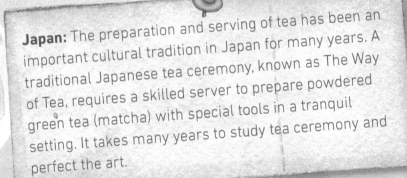

JAPAN

Cucumber Salad (Sunomono)

The name of this dish literally means "vinegared thing" in Japanese. It is a simple, refreshing and very traditional dish. Prepare Sunomono just before you plan to eat as it is best when it is fresh.

Cucumbers are a very common ingredient in Japanese food, prepared in salads, sashimi and sushi. Known as Kyuri in Japanese, Japanese Cucumbers are long and slender, and don't have any developed seeds. Visit your local Asian market to find these cucumbers if you can, but keep in mind regular cucumbers will work just fine if you can't find Kyuri.

Hirosaki Castle, built over 400 years ago!

Fishpole Bamboo - Phyllostachys aurea

187

Cucumber Salad (Sunomono)

1 In a medium bowl, whisk together rice vinegar, sugar, soy sauce, and salt until all of the ingredients dissolve. Chill.

2 Clean the cucumbers well and cut into coin-like, very thin slices. Lay out the slices in a colander, lightly salt, and let them sit for 15 minutes. Rinse the salt off and drain.

3 Mix the sliced cucumbers with the chilled liquid mixture, then chill for an additional 15 minutes or so. Sprinkle sesame seeds on each dish when you serve.

A TIP JUST FOR KIDS!

While this is a very traditional dish, there are some fun variations. Search online and find alternative recipes using wakame seaweed, cellophane noodles and seafood.

Ideas for Continued Learning

Explore: Japan's land mass is made up of 6,852 islands! Research what the names of the main 5 (largest) islands are.

Watch: Experience an ancient form of Japanese theatrical art. Search Youtube for "Kabuki Theater." Tell someone about your experience watching it for the first time.

INGREDIENTS

6 tablespoons unseasoned rice vinegar

1 tablespoon sugar

1 teaspoon soy sauce

1 teaspoon salt, plus more for sprinkling on cucumbers

1 Japanese cucumber

1 teaspoon sesame seeds for garnish

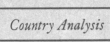

JAPAN

Capital City / Tokyo
Nation Language / Japanese
Population / 126,317,000
Currency / Japanese Yen

Japan is located in an area known as the ring of fire, a zone surrounding the Pacific Ocean that experiences many earthquakes and volcanic eruptions. Indeed, there are more than 1000 earthquakes in Japan each year, but advancements in building technology have been made so major damage is minimized.

Momotarō "The Peach Boy"

Many years ago in ancient Japan, there lived an old man and woman who had no children. Each day the man would go into the mountains to cut firewood, and the woman would go to the river to wash laundry. Their lives were happy, but relatively uneventful.

One day while washing laundry, the old woman spied a very large peach floating toward her. She pulled the peach from the water to surprise her husband with a delicious dinner. When she raised the knife to cut into the peach she heard a gentle plea from within, "Please don't eat me!" At that moment, the peach burst open and a beautiful baby boy jumped out. They couple named him Momotarō (Peach Boy) and raised him as their own.

The baby grew into a young man with many athletic gifts. He was strong and very intelligent, and he wanted to give back to the community who raised him. "Mother and Father, I want to travel to Ogre Island to defeat the ogres that plague us. I will bring their riches home so all of us can prosper."

Momotarō journeyed to Ogre Island, making friends along the way. Each of his new friends bestowed him with special gifts that enhanced his physical and mental abilities. Because of these gifts and the friendships he built, he was eventually able to vanquish the evil ogres and bring their riches home to his community. Because of his courageousness, Momotarō is celebrated everywhere in Japan to this day.

Getting to Know Japan

Fill in the missing information on this page. You can find the correct answers in your copy of *The Cultured Chef,* or search online to retrieve the information needed.

Capital City:

Country Population:

Language:

Google Japan's flag and use as reference to color the drawing below.

JAPAN

Japan - The Great Wave

The woodblock print titled
"The Great Wave off Kanagawa"
is perhaps one of the most famous
Japanese works of art. Created by
the artist Hokusai in 1823, the print
measures 10x14 inches.

White-naped Crane - *Antigone vipio*

Hanok is the term given to traditional Korean houses. Korean architecture puts much consideration into how a home is positioned in relation to it's surroundings. There is, however, a wide variety of housing styles as found anywhere else.

the republic of korea

Bibimbap

Bibimbap is a Korean rice dish that means "Mixed rice." It is a very common dish that can be served many different ways, likely depending upon the ingredients a household has available. Around 100 years old, Bibimbap is based on a much older recipe (Goldongban) that folks prepared on the eve of the lunar new year. It provided them a way to clean out their pantries and throw whatever they had into their rice bowl.

A NOTE ABOUT BIBIMBAP:

There are very many recipes for Bibimbap, and most include a bit more spice, fried rice, and fermented vegetables. The recipe I've presented here is a simplified version suitable for kids, but please feel free to research alternative recipes if you'd like.

There is a Korean tradition of giving a hand fan as a special gift during the Dano Festival each year. Giving a hand fan is an important way of showing you care for someone. It is believed the fans were invented in Korea by a Buddhist monk many, many years ago (during the Goryeo Dynasty) and artisans continue to produce them today. Fans play an important role in ceremonies and theatrical performances in their culture.

Bibimbap

1 Assemble all prepared ingredients. Place sliced thin strips of cucumber in 1 cup of lightly salted water to soak for 20 minutes. Drain and pat dry.

2 Over medium-high heat in a nonstick skillet, heat ½ tablespoon of sesame oil and 1 tablespoon of soy sauce, then add spinach. Cook until spinach begins to soften, but maintains its color. Remove and set aside.

3 In the same skillet, repeat this process with each of the following ingredients individually; carrots, zucchini, and mushrooms. (Use ½ tablespoon of sesame oil and 1 tablespoon of soy sauce each time) You want to heat and soften each ingredient, but not overcook them.

4 In the same skillet, heat 1 tablespoon of sesame oil and 1 tablespoon of soy sauce, then add the strips of beef. Sauté until the meat is no longer pink. Remove from the pan and set aside.

5 Portion the rice out into 4 bowls, arranging each of the ingredients in a circular fashion around the bowl. Place the fried egg on top if desired, then garnish with sesame seeds.

A TIP JUST FOR KIDS!

While this is a very traditional dish, there are some fun variations. Search online and find alternative recipes using wakame seaweed, cellophane noodles and seafood.

Ideas for Continued Learning

Watch: Search "Buchaechum" on Youtube to watch a traditional Korean folk dance by a group of female dancers using fans.

Research: The Korean Peninsula is divided in half, with The Democratic Peoples Republic of Korea (or North Korea) to the north. Find articles about North Korea in the news and discuss as a family.

INGREDIENTS

1 cup lightly salted water

2 cups cooked medium grain rice

1 large cucumber
  (sliced into thin strips)

1 ½ cups bean sprouts (parboiled)

1 ½ cups shredded spinach

2 carrots (julienned)

4 shiitake mushrooms (sliced)

2 cups zucchini (sliced into thin strips)

3 tablespoons sesame oil

5 tablespoons low sodium soy sauce

1 lb beef sirloin, skirt, or ribeye
  (cut into strips)

4 fried eggs (optional)

Sesame seeds as a garnish

194

THE REPUBLIC OF KOREA

Capital City / Seoul	
Nation Language / Korean	
Population / 51,708,098	
Currency / Korean Republic Won	

The Korean Peninsula is a 750-mile long peninsula that was ruled by the Japanese for 35 years until 1945 when they were defeated in World War II. Five years later the Korean war broke out and the Korean Peninsula was divided in half, into North and South Korea. It remains divided to this day.

The Story of Heungboo and Nolbu

Once upon a time, there were two brothers named Heungboo and Nolbu. The two brothers couldn't be any more different from one another. Nolbu held many riches but was also very greedy. Heungboo was very poor, but he was kind and generous.

Heungboo found an injured sparrow while working in his garden one day. He took kindness upon the poor creature by taking it into his home and nursing it back to health. "Fly away little bird, you have a second chance at life," he exclaimed as he watched the bird ascend into the clouds above. The bird repaid his kindness 7 days later when she returned with three magical gourd seeds. The seeds sprouted and eventually ripened, yielding a fortune in gold coins.

Nolbu flew into a jealous rage, wanting gold coins of his own. He found a similar sparrow, caged it for many weeks with little food or water, then released it when he felt the bird had suffered enough. Surprisingly, this sparrow returned with three seeds as well and Nolbu planted them immediately. When it came time to harvest his riches, a brood of devils burst forth from the gourds and ravaged his home and family. The devils left him with nothing, because it doesn't pay to be greedy.

Getting to Know the Republic of Korea

Fill in the missing information on this page. You can find the correct answers in your copy of *The Cultured Chef*, or search online to retrieve the information needed.

Capital City:

Country Population:

Language:

....

Google the Republic of Korea's flag and use as reference to color the drawing below.

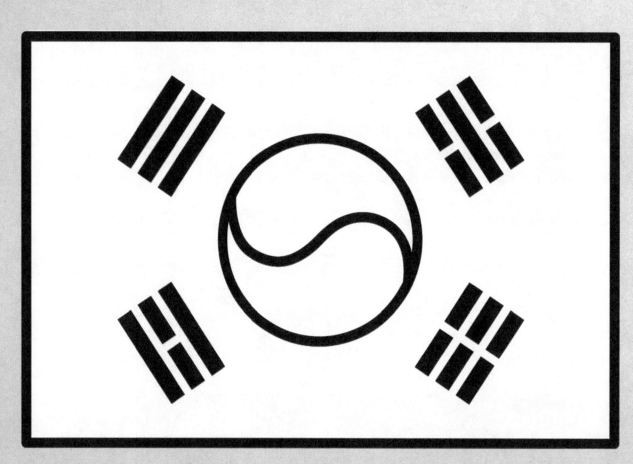

Color the World!

Korea - Sejong The Great

This statue of King Sejong is located at the Gwanghwamun Plaza in Seoul, South Korea. Sejong the Great is considered to be one of Korea's most famous historical figures. This statue was unveiled in 2009.

This twisted teardrop pattern (now known worldwide as Paisley) traces its history back to Persia around 220 AD. The design represents the Cypress tree, which many see as a symbol of eternity and life. The design is now commonly found on carpets, curtains, jewelry and other works of art

IRAN

PERSIAN MEATBALLS (KOOFTEH)

This meatball dish is one of the more complicated recipes in the cookbook, but it is definitely worth trying. Maybe now is a good time to consult the Shopping for A Global Kitchen section of the book, and get to know your local international market. This recipe calls for a lot of fun spices you might not already have in your pantry.

It's time to get out your rulers, kids! While our meatballs are only going to be an inch or so in diameter, some Persian meatballs (a recipe called Tabriz köftesi) are often as big as 7.5 inches in diameter! Can you even imagine a meatball that big?

Date Palm - *Phoenix dactylifera*

The camel is a useful beast of burden that is well-suited to living in the hot and dry climate of the Middle East. They are raised to provide meat and milk, as well as transportation and heavy work such as carrying loads and pulling things. The camel has been raised as a domesticated animal for several thousand years.

Arabian Camel -
Camelus dromedaries

PERSIAN MEATBALLS (KOOFTEH)

1 Mix ground beef, onion, cilantro, turmeric, 1 teaspoon salt, sumac & coriander seeds.

2 Form ground beef into small 1-inch cocktail size meatballs and set aside on a plate until all of the meatballs are formed.

3 Heat olive oil in large sauté pan over medium heat. Add meatballs in batches if the pan isn't large enough. Do not overcrowd the pan. Brown meatballs on all sides.

4 While meatballs are cooking, evenly sprinkle remaining 1 teaspoon turmeric and 1 teaspoon lemon pepper on the meatballs. Pour lime juice over them, reduce heat to medium-low and simmer for 10 minutes. Then pour tomato sauce over meatballs, and add cherry tomatoes, distributing evenly in pan.

5 Sprinkle sauce with remaining 1 teaspoon salt, dried dill and remaining 1/2 teaspoon lemon pepper. Reduce heat to low, cover, and simmer for 10 minutes.

6 Transfer meatballs and sauce to a large serving bowl. Serve hot over basmati rice.

A TIP JUST FOR KIDS!

If you really want to have fun with this recipe, consider placing a piece of dried fruit at the center of each of your meatballs. You can use dried plums, dates or raisins. Who doesn't like a fun surprise when trying a new dish?

Ideas for Continued Learning

Draw: You've learned about the Boteh Jegheh pattern known as Paisley. Google image search for "Free Printable Paisley Coloring Pages" and enjoy making colorful patterns.

Research: The Arabian Camel (Also known as Dromedary) has one hump. But there are Camels with two humps as well. Research Bactrian Camels and see if you can discover how else they are different.

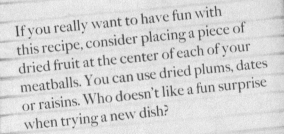

INGREDIENTS

1 pound ground beef
3/4 cup onions, chopped
1/2 cup chopped cilantro
2 teaspoons turmeric, divided
2 teaspoons Himalayan salt
1 teaspoon sumac
1 teaspoon coriander seeds
4 tablespoons olive oil
1 teaspoon lemon pepper, divided
2 cups tomato sauce
2 tablespoons lime juice
12 cherry tomatoes
1 teaspoon dried dill

IRAN

Capital City / Tehran	
Nation Language / Persian	
Population / 82,531,700	
Currency / Iranian Rial	

There are many thousands of villages in Iran. While each village is unique, there are a number of characteristics that make them similar. A typical village has a mosque (a place of worship), a bathhouse for bathing, and a public market. Many of the people living in Iran live much as their ancestors did 100 years prior, farming or making a living as an artisan.

THE HUMA BIRD

A mythical bird of Iranian legends and fables, the Huma Bird never rests on the ground. Instead, she circles high above, watching for opportunities to bestow gifts on those below.

Exhausted from a long day of unsuccessfully looking for work, a peasant man sought shade under a date palm. The clatter of wagons and tradesmen walking in both directions didn't prevent him from falling into a deep sleep. High above, a Huma Bird drifted gracefully in the wind's current. She noticed the man below, in ragged clothing, and she took pity on him. "I will give him a golden egg so his mind won't be clouded with worry."

When the man awoke, he found the golden egg sitting next to him and he was overcome with emotion. "Now I can feed my family!" Unsure of the value of the egg, the man returned to the market and asked a merchant for guidance. "How much will you give me for this golden egg," the peasant inquired. "I'll give you one day's wage for this egg," said the merchant. "That will be enough to buy your family a wholesome dinner, and buy several small gifts to show your love."

The merchant was an unfair man, as he knew the true value of the egg. "Why don't you return where you found this egg, and come back tomorrow with another?" the merchant suggested. "I will pay you twice as much tomorrow."

The Huma Bird indeed returned the next day, and she left yet another golden egg. But the peasant became greedy. He waited, with one eye open, only pretending to be asleep. "If I catch this bird, perhaps the merchant will pay me triple!" So when the Huma Bird began her ascent, the peasant reached up and grasped onto her leg tightly. The peasant couldn't have made a bigger mistake. The bird quickly vanished, as well as the golden egg laying beside him. In a matter of two days, the peasant lost two fortunes due to his greed and ignorance.

Getting to Know Iran

Fill in the missing information on this page. You can find the correct answers in your copy of *The Cultured Chef,* or search online to retrieve the information needed.

Capital City:

Country Population:

Language:

Google Iran's flag and use as reference to color the drawing below.

IRAN

Iran - Persepolis

Persepolis is a well-preserved
ancient city that is now an architectual
treasure. Great halls, intricate pillars like
the one pictured here, and beautiful stairways
exist to this day.

The Flora and Fauna of Asia

Asia is the largest continent of the planet, in land mass and population as well. The Asian continent includes a whopping 48 countries. The continent is located mainly in the eastern hemisphere and in the northern hemisphere. In Asia, there are monkeys, tigers, Asian elephants and many other animals.

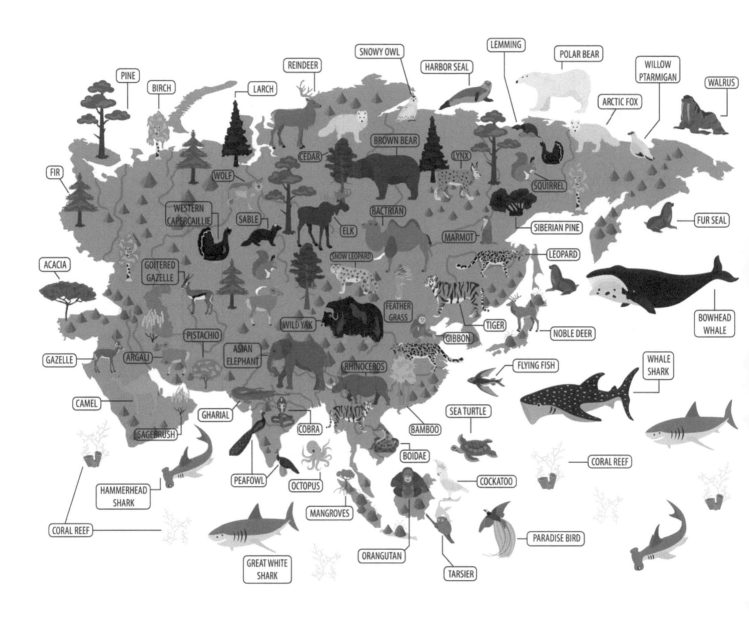

Animals
of Asia

There is a lot to consider when learning about animals of the world. Different animals are suited to different climates, and have particular tastes when it comes to the food they need to survive. A penguin won't feel very much at home on the beach in Miami, Florida, would it?

Select an animal from the previous page about Asia and write a short report below. Where does the animal live? What does the animal like to eat? Are there any other facts about this animal you find interesting?

Use the space below to write down interesting facts about the animal you have chosen.

ASIA

"Cross a river in a crowd and the crocodile won't eat you."

Madagascan Proverb, Author Unknown

AFRICA

EGYPT - MOROCCO - KENYA ZIMBABWE - NIGERIA - SOUTH AFRICA

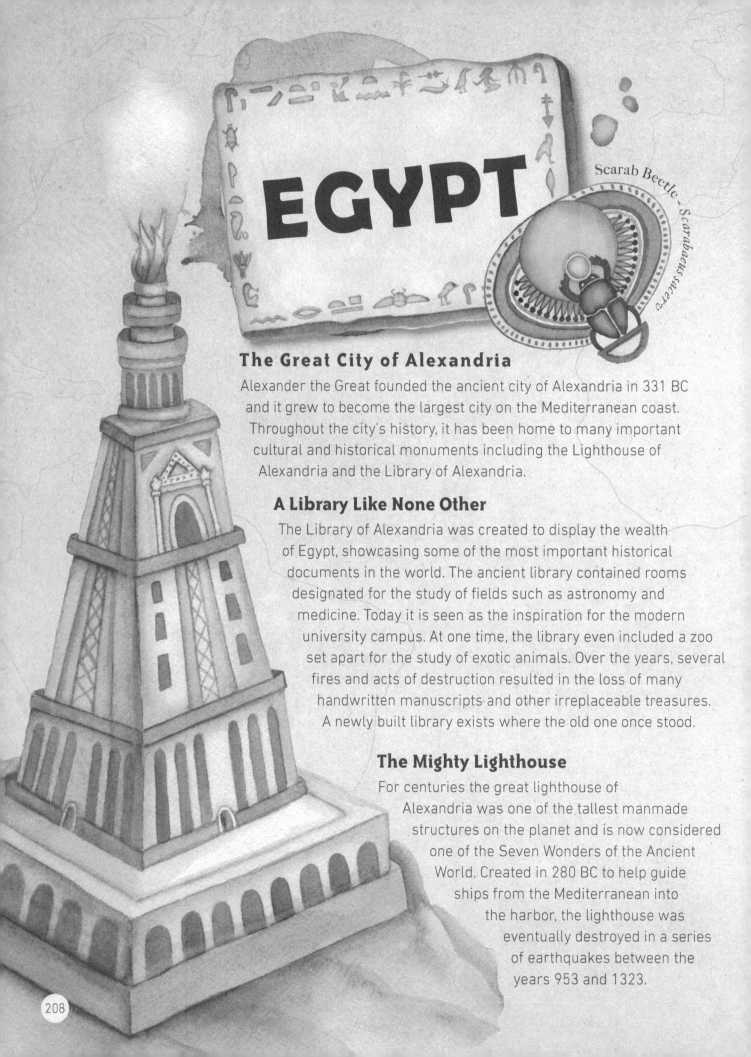

EGYPT

Scarab Beetle ~ Scarabaeus sacer

The Great City of Alexandria

Alexander the Great founded the ancient city of Alexandria in 331 BC and it grew to become the largest city on the Mediterranean coast. Throughout the city's history, it has been home to many important cultural and historical monuments including the Lighthouse of Alexandria and the Library of Alexandria.

A Library Like None Other

The Library of Alexandria was created to display the wealth of Egypt, showcasing some of the most important historical documents in the world. The ancient library contained rooms designated for the study of fields such as astronomy and medicine. Today it is seen as the inspiration for the modern university campus. At one time, the library even included a zoo set apart for the study of exotic animals. Over the years, several fires and acts of destruction resulted in the loss of many handwritten manuscripts and other irreplaceable treasures. A newly built library exists where the old one once stood.

The Mighty Lighthouse

For centuries the great lighthouse of Alexandria was one of the tallest manmade structures on the planet and is now considered one of the Seven Wonders of the Ancient World. Created in 280 BC to help guide ships from the Mediterranean into the harbor, the lighthouse was eventually destroyed in a series of earthquakes between the years 953 and 1323.

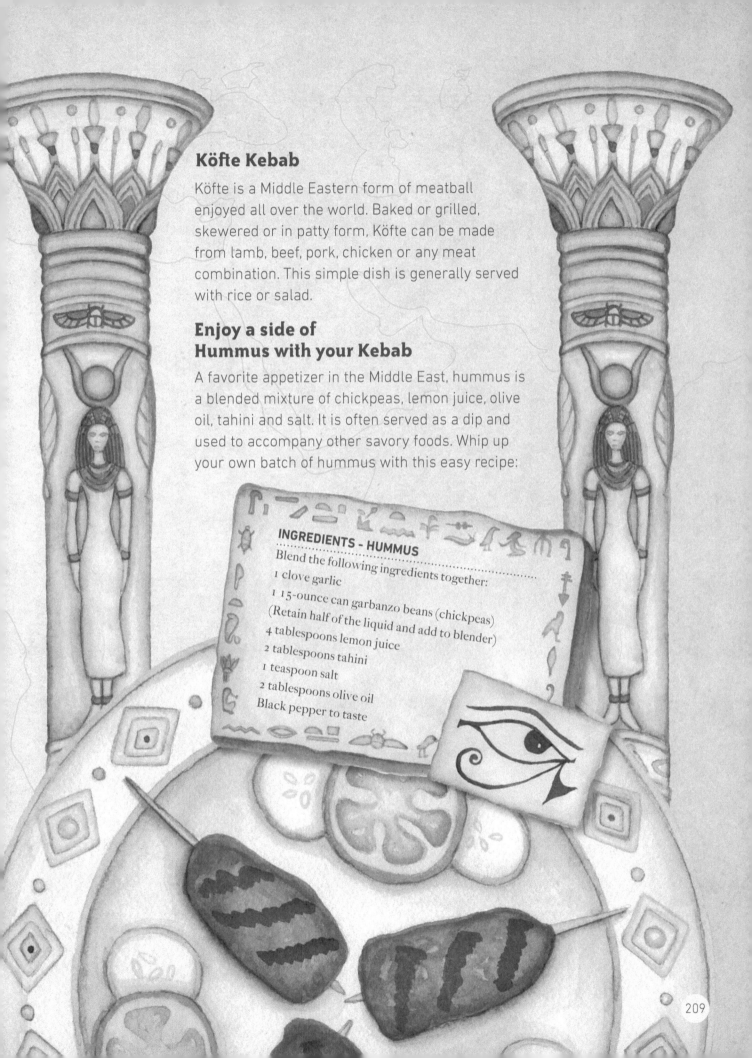

Köfte Kebab

Köfte is a Middle Eastern form of meatball enjoyed all over the world. Baked or grilled, skewered or in patty form, Köfte can be made from lamb, beef, pork, chicken or any meat combination. This simple dish is generally served with rice or salad.

Enjoy a side of Hummus with your Kebab

A favorite appetizer in the Middle East, hummus is a blended mixture of chickpeas, lemon juice, olive oil, tahini and salt. It is often served as a dip and used to accompany other savory foods. Whip up your own batch of hummus with this easy recipe:

INGREDIENTS - HUMMUS

Blend the following ingredients together:

1 clove garlic

1 15-ounce can garbanzo beans (chickpeas)
(Retain half of the liquid and add to blender)

4 tablespoons lemon juice

2 tablespoons tahini

1 teaspoon salt

2 tablespoons olive oil

Black pepper to taste

Köfte Kebab

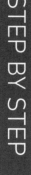

1 Prepare bamboo skewers by soaking them in water for 20 minutes.

2 Mash garlic and salt into a paste using a mortar and pestle. (You can be creative if you don't have a mortar and pestle; try using a rolling pin on a cutting board or the back of a fork.)

3 Mix the garlic and salt paste with ground beef and lamb. Add onion, parsley, black pepper, lemon zest and the rest of the spices. Mix well.

4 Form the mixture into 20 balls. Insert the skewer and flatten the ball into somewhat of an oval shape. The Köfte should be a little off center on the skewer, leaving room to handle later. Place on a foil-lined baking pan and refrigerate at least 30 minutes (up to 12 hours).

5 Preheat oven to 350 degrees Fahrenheit and bake for 30 minutes. Serve with rice or salad.

A TIP JUST FOR KIDS!

"Köfte taste amazing with tzatziki yogurt sauce! You can find that recipe in the Greece section of our cookbook."

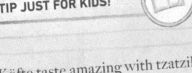

Ideas for Continued Learning

Explore: The Nile River is the longest river in the world measuring 4,132 miles. Discover why this river is so important to Egypt, and much of Africa.

Watch: Search Youtube for a video about Tutankhamen (or King Tut) the world famous pharaoh from the year 1342.

INGREDIENTS

4 cloves garlic, minced
1 teaspoon salt
1/2 pound ground lamb
1/2 pound ground beef
1/2 cup white onion, finely grated
1/2 cup chopped fresh parsley
1/4 teaspoon ground black pepper
Zest of 1 lemon
20 bamboo skewers

OPTIONAL SPICES

1 tablespoon ground coriander
1 teaspoon ground cumin
½ teaspoon allspice
¼ teaspoon cinnamon
¼ teaspoon paprika
¼ teaspoon ground ginger

EGYPT

Capital City /	Cairo
Nation Language /	Arabic
Population /	85,550,000
Currency /	Egyptian pound

Egypt *receives irrigation to its farmlands thanks to The Nile River, a very important natural resource. More than 96 percent of Egypt is considered desert because the country receives less than one inch of rain a year.*

Anubis: He Who is Upon His Mountain

Egyptian mythology details the lives of the gods who helped the ancient Egyptians understand their world better. There were more than two thousand gods who held many responsibilities in all planes of existence. Learn more about one of our favorites, Anubis.

The god of funerals, Anubis was responsible for preparing the soul for the afterlife. He watched over the mummification process to make sure it all went smoothly and assessed those passing through the underworld by placing their hearts on the Scale of Justice.

The Egyptians noticed jackals hanging around the graveyards when their loved ones were recently laid to rest. The people assumed that Anubis favored the pesky creatures, so they began associating the jackal with him. To this day, Anubis is depicted with the head of a jackal and the body of a man.

Pandalus borealis: *One of the many gifts of the Nile River is a weedy plant called Papyrus. This plant has been used throughout Egyptian history to create everything from baskets and sandals to rope and paper.*

Getting to Know Egypt

Fill in the missing information on this page. You can find the correct answers in your copy of *The Cultured Chef,* or search online to retrieve the information needed.

Capital City:

Country Population:

Language:

Google Egypt's flag and use as reference to color the drawing below.

EGYPT

Egypt - The Citadel of Cairo

Construction began on this beautiful Egyptian fortress in 1176. The building has been used as an armed fortress, a palace for rulers, as well as a religious site. The Citadel of Cairo is one of the most recognized landmarks in Egypt.

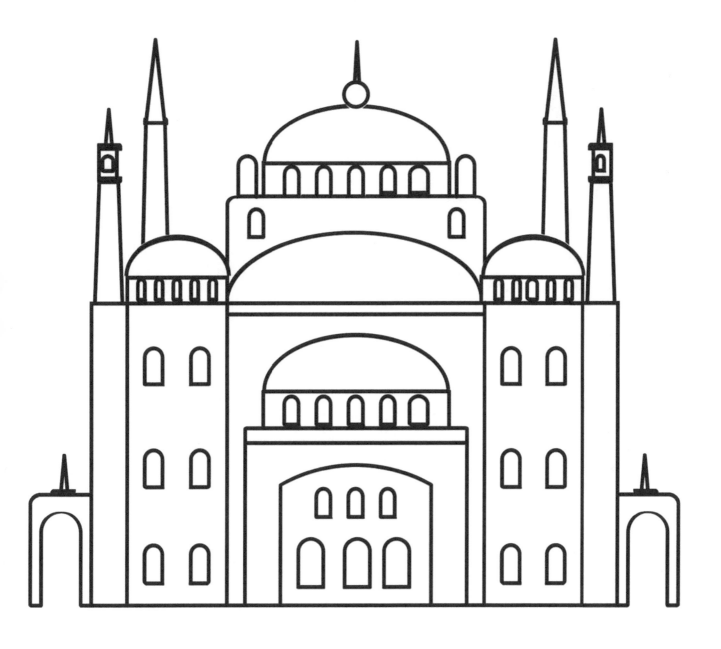

MOROCCO

The market of Marrakech is like no other place in the world. Rich with a colorful array of pottery, clothing and spices, the market is a feast for the eyes. It was built in the medina quarter (the central historic part of the city) and has changed little over the thousands of years the market has operated. For this reason, the location has been declared a site of cultural and historical importance.

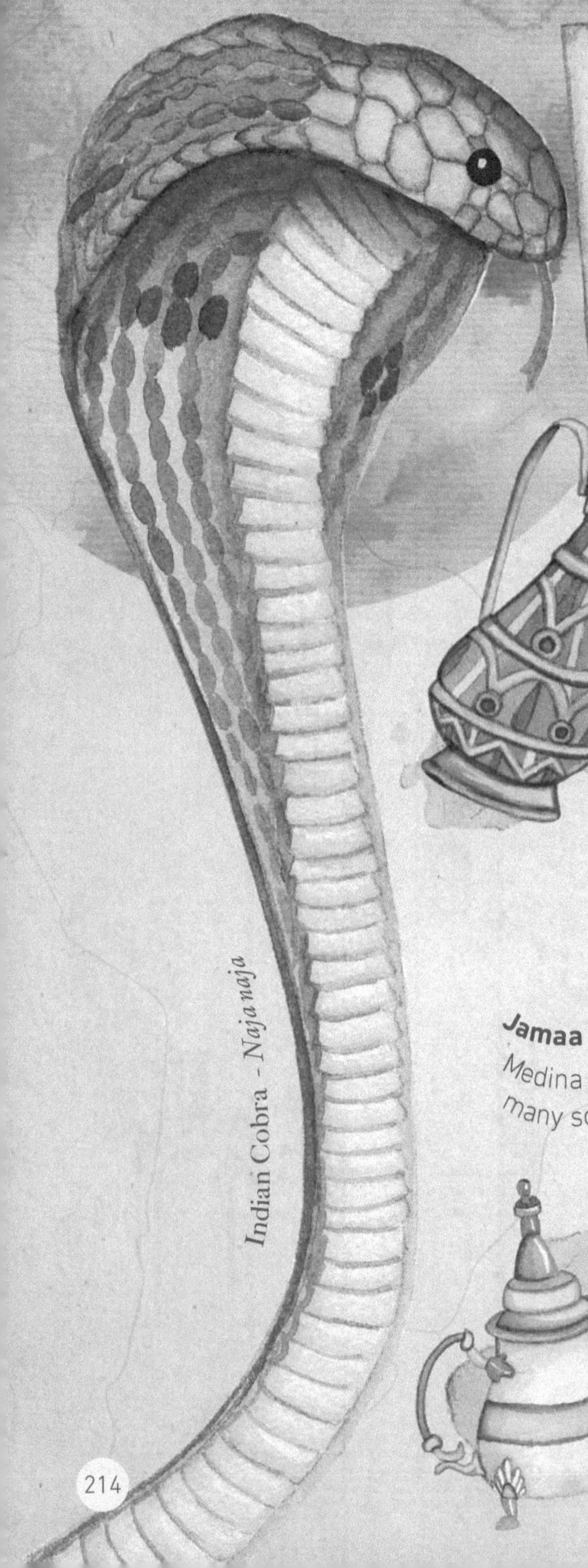

Souk: An open-air marketplace, or Bazaar filled with market stalls offering many different products.

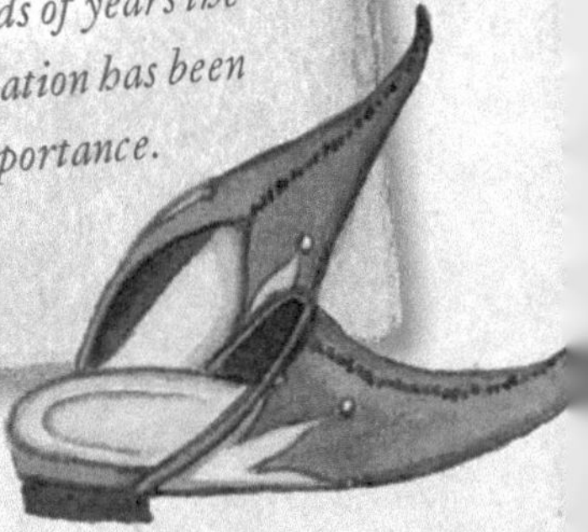

words you should know

Jamaa el Fna: The large public square in the Medina of Marrakech, around which are situated many souks.

Riad: Historic Moroccan house with many rooms surrounding an internal courtyard. There are many Riad in the Medina of Marrakech.

Indian Cobra - *Naja naja*

214

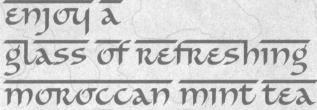

enjoy a glass of refreshing moroccan mint tea

- In a medium size kettle, boil at least 4 cups of water (some will evaporate).

- Combine 2 cups hot water, mint, green tea, orange blossom water and sugar in a large teapot and let steep for at least 3 minutes.

- Place a sprig of mint in a medium size drinking glass. Pour tea mixture through a strainer, filling the glass. Enjoy.

INGREDIENTS

1 tablespoon gunpowder green tea leaves
1 large handful fresh spearmint leaves, washed
2 cups boiling water
¼ cup sugar
¼ teaspoon orange blossom water

Mint

Mentha spicata

The Hand of Fatima

This ancient design was originally found in Mesopotamian art and was known as hamsa. It was considered a sign of protection and is found in the paintings, artwork and jewelry of various cultures and religions. Moroccans in Islamic culture called it The Hand of Fatima, a reference to the Prophet Muhammad's daughter Fatima. In Buddhism, the right-hand open palm signifies the Buddha's gesture of teaching and protection.

stained glass cookies

Even though most Moroccan families serve seasonal fruits after a meal, you know it is time for dessert when the mint tea and cookies arrive at the table. Pastries dripping with honey and smelling of exotic spices like cinnamon, ginger and mint linger heavy in the air.

In every region, patisseries (pastry shops) and market stalls overflow with colorful and aromatic cookies of every shape and size. Moroccans take pride in the food they prepare, both in flavor and presentation, and visitors always find something new to love when dessert is served.

215

Stained Glass Cookies

1 In a medium bowl, beat butter and sugar with an electric mixer on medium speed until the mixture is fluffy, 2-3 minutes. Continue beating and add the egg, vanilla and salt. Reduce speed and add flour until the mixture is combined. Do not over-mix.

2 Divide dough in half, shaping into two rounds. Wrap in plastic and refrigerate until firm.

3 Heat oven to 350 degrees Fahrenheit.

4 Lightly flour your work surface then roll out each piece of dough to 1/8-inch thickness. Cut the dough into interesting shapes using a 2-inch cookie cutter, then place them on a parchment-lined baking sheet. Make sure to space the cookies at least 1-inch apart. Using a second ¾- to 1-inch cookie cutter, cut out the centers from each cookie.

5 Spoon ½ to 1 teaspoon of the crushed candy (depending on the size of the cutout) into the center of each cookie. Bake until the edges are just golden, 7-9 minutes. Cook on the baking sheets for at least 5 minutes, then transfer to wire racks to cool completely.

6 Be sure to store the cookies between wax paper sheets in an airtight container.

A TIP JUST FOR KIDS!

I enjoyed these delicious cookies, Sablés à la Confiture, in Marrakech when I was exploring Morocco several years ago. You'll find variations of these cookies in many cultures, but it was the French who introduced them to Morocco.

Ideas for Continued Learning

Draw: A Riad is a Moroccan version of an American mansion with many rooms and features. Search Youtube for "Tour of Moroccan Riad" to see the architecture and style of these beautiful homes. Understand, not everyone lives like this. Perhaps research "Traditional Moroccan Homes" to see the variety of housing in the country.

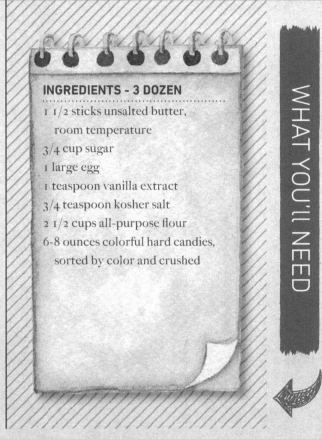

INGREDIENTS - 3 DOZEN

1 1/2 sticks unsalted butter, room temperature

3/4 cup sugar

1 large egg

1 teaspoon vanilla extract

3/4 teaspoon kosher salt

2 1/2 cups all-purpose flour

6-8 ounces colorful hard candies, sorted by color and crushed

MOROCCO

Capital City /	Rabat
Nation Language /	Arabic
Population /	32,649,130
Currency /	Moroccan dirhams

Morocco *is situated in the northwest corner of Africa, with the majority of the country's population living in the coastal cities of Fez, Casablanca and Marrakech. The Atlas Mountains and the Sahara Desert dominate the Moroccan landscape.*

the spices of morocco

Moroccan cooking is known for the many spices that are used to enhance the flavor and fragrance of the food. Spices and herbs are such an important part of Moroccan cuisine, an overwhelming number of market stalls specialize in providing "just right" blends perfect for creating sweet and savory dishes. Below are some of the most common spices used in Morocco.

Cumin: The seeds of the plant *Cuminum cyminum* are used as a spice for their distinctive flavor and aroma. It has been used since ancient times and serves as a staple for many Moroccan homes.

Turmeric: Though it is typically used in a powdered, dry form, fresh turmeric *Curcuma longa* can also be used much like ginger. Turmeric was once known as Indian Saffron because it was cheaper and more widely available than the real saffron.

Paprika: A spice made from ground, dried peppers *Capsicum annuum*, paprika is primarily used to season and color rice, stew and soups.

Saffron

Crocus sativus

Getting to Know Morocco

Fill in the missing information on this page. You can find the correct answers in your copy of *The Cultured Chef,* or search online to retrieve the information needed.

Capital City:

Country Population:

Language:

Google Morocco's flag and use as reference to color the drawing below.

Morocco

Color the World!

Morocco - Argan Oil

The Argan tree is native to Morocco. Kernals are harvested from the fruit that yields a special oil used in cooking and cosmetics. Moroccans dip bread in argan oil at breakfast, or drizzle the oil on their couscous and pasta.

HERBS AND SPICES OF THE WORLD

For much of recorded history, world civilizations have used herbs and spices for cooking, cleaning and in medicine. Explorers have traveled far and wide to find these prized resources, even going to war over them!

Do you know the difference between herbs and spices? Herbs can be enjoyed fresh or dried and include the leafy parts of a plant, whereas spices are derived from the dried stems, bark, roots, nuts or seeds of a plant. Both herbs and spices give global cuisines their unique and delicious flavors.

Ginseng: *Panax ginseng* (China) Grown only in the cooler climates of the Northern Hemisphere, ginseng is harvested for its thick and fleshy roots, called rhizomes. It is used to make tea, soups and sauces and to flavor vegetables and pork. One variety, Panax quinquefolius, is native to the Appalachian region of the United States.

Star Anise: *Illicium verum* (Vietnam and China) Star anise is the small, woody fruit of a tree in the Magnolia family. Although it smells very much like a spice called anise, the two plants are completely unrelated. Star anise is used to prepare Vietnamese Pho (a noodle and beef broth soup) as well as Chinese Marbled Eggs.

Lavender: *Lavandula angustifolia* (France and England) Lavender is a highly aromatic flower that is used for cooking, potpourri, cosmetics, cleaning products and much more. Originally grown in England and France, lavender is fairly easy to grow and can be cultivated almost everywhere in the world.

Saffron: *Crocus sativus* (Greece) One of the world's most expensive spices, saffron is used in rice and meat dishes throughout India, Europe, the Middle East, Turkey and elsewhere. Because each crocus blossom only provides a few fragrant strands every season, there is a high demand for the spice, with prices ranging from $500-5,000.00 per pound.

Cinnamon: *Cinnamomum verum* (India and Sri Lanka) Several tree varieties within the same family produce an aromatic bark that is harvested and sold as cinnamon. Cinnamon is one of the most recognizable spices around the world due to its unique scent. Cooks use the spice primarily in desserts, syrups and curries.

Vanilla: *Vanilla planifolia* (Mexico) Vanilla comes from the fruit of an exotic orchid vine that originates in parts of Mexico and Guatemala. The fruit pods, commonly called beans, are harvested and cured by hand. Vanilla is used most often in desserts and to enhance the flavor of other ingredients such as chocolate, coffee or caramel.

KENYA

African Bush Elephant -
Loxodonta africana

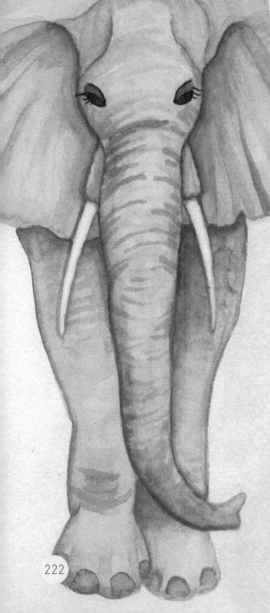

Acacia Tree

There are few scenes as iconic as the Acacia tree far off in the distance of the Serengeti plains of Kenya and Tanzania, with the sun setting in the background and a tall giraffe feeding on the nutritious leaves of the tree.

Fever Tree - Acacia xanthophloea

The Natural Beauty of Kenya

Kenya has a diverse landscape stretching from the Indian Ocean inward toward the endless plains of the Serengeti. The source of the Nile River can be found in Lake Victoria with its world famous Nile crocodiles. The country's namesake, Mount Kenya stretches over 17,000 feet high, making it the second highest peak in Africa.

Kenya is home to some of the most incredible animals in the world, including elephants, lions, giraffes, zebras, antelope, wildebeests and many more. Sadly, hunting and construction in natural habitats once set aside for the animals threatens their very existence. The government and many animal rights organizations are now working to ensure the animals will be around for many years to come.

Githeri –
Kenyan Corn
and Beans

Kenyan cuisine is relatively easy to prepare, both in terms of the number of ingredients and the time it takes to cook. Originating from the Kikuyu tribe in central Kenya, Githeri is one of the most traditional dishes prepared throughout the country.

Traditional Githeri is comprised primarily of corn, beans and tomatoes, making it a very nutritious dish. Historically, Githeri was prepared in clay pots over fire, a process that took many hours. Thanks to modern conveniences the meal can be prepared in no time at all.

Ninapenda twiga, simba, na punda milia

Masai Giraffe – Giraffa camelopardalis tippelskirchi

The
Maasai Giraffe:
The graceful giraffe is the tallest mammal on the earth and is found in the plains of Kenya. With a neck that stretches almost seven feet tall, the giraffe is able to reach high above other animals to eat the leaves of the Acacia trees.

223

Githeri – Kenyan Corn and Beans

1 Heat the vegetable oil in a large pot and sauté the onions and garlic over medium heat until they are lightly cooked, about 3 minutes.

2 Add the curry powder and cook for another minute.

3 Add the kale and reduce the heat to low. Cook, stirring with a wooden spoon until the kale softens, about 10 minutes.

4 Add the tomatoes, corn and beans and simmer another 10 minutes. Add the reserved tomato juice and continue cooking until heated through.

5 Season to your taste with salt and pepper then serve and share! Feel free to personalize your Githeri by adding a few teaspoons of your favorite dried herb such as oregano, thyme or sage.

A TIP JUST FOR KIDS!

" This is a pretty easy recipe to make together as a family. I enjoy helping my little brother prepare Githeri because he can easily measure and pour the ingredients. And he loves stirring the pot while it's cooking!"

Ideas for Continued Learning

Consider: Learn about safaris in Kenya. Search Youtube for "African Sarari" videos. Discuss the pros and cons of African safaris. How are they important for the economy, and how are they perhaps not so good for the animals?

INGREDIENTS

1 tablespoon vegetable oil

1 large onion, chopped

3 cloves of garlic, minced

1 tablespoon curry powder

1 large bunch fresh kale, chopped

1 28-ounce can of whole tomatoes, drained, reserve the juice

1 15-ounce can whole kernel corn

2 cups of cooked beans, any type, drained and rinsed

Juice of 1 lemon

KENYA

Capital City /	Nairobi
Nation Language /	Swahili
Population /	44,354,000
Currency /	Kenyan Shilling

Kenya is home to more than 450 of some of the earliest fossils belonging to humans, found in the Turkana Basin in Kenya. This evidence leads many scientists to believe the region may have been the birthplace of the original humans.

The Kenyan Maasai

The Maasai are one of the most recognizable and prolific tribes in East Africa. Despite their proximity to modern communities, they still maintain most of their traditional ways and live like their ancestors have for more than 500 years. What started as a small group of warriors with a herd of cattle many years ago has become a large group numbering nearly 900,000 people.

Although the Maasai are known as fierce warriors, the cattle they raise are their most important priority. Raising cattle is an important aspect of the Maasai culture because they believe the rain god Enkai gave all the cattle of the world to them. As you can imagine, this has caused some problems in the past when Maasai found other tribes with cattle. They assumed that the cows must have been stolen from them.

The men of the tribe are responsible for tending the cattle and building thorny fences around the village for protection. Women play an important role in the tribe, having the responsibility of building their homes. Known as Inkajijik, the round huts are built of small tree poles, branches, grass and mud. The entire structure is then covered with cow dung, which when dried, protects and waterproofs the home.

Maasai women are world-famous bead workers, capable of creating vibrantly colored necklaces and clothing. The women of the tribe express their identity and position in society through body painting, piercings, beaded jewelry and brightly colored clothing.

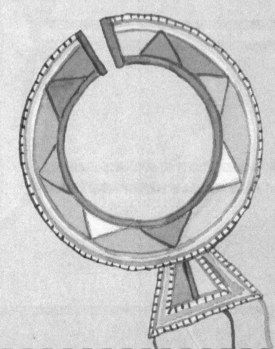

Getting to Know Kenya

Fill in the missing information on this page. You can find the correct answers in your copy of *The Cultured Chef*, or search online to retrieve the information needed.

Capital City:

Country Population:

Language:

Google Kenya's flag and use as reference to color the drawing below.

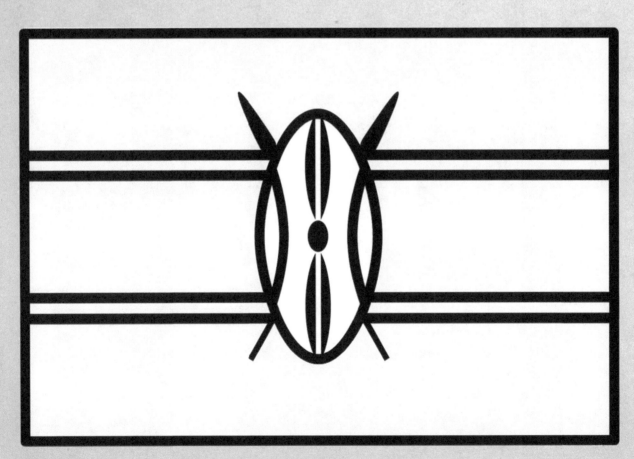

Kenya - Maasai Warrior

The Maasai people of Kenya are a semi-nomadic tribe who continue to live in their traditional ways. This Maasai warrior is preparing to leave his village on a walkabout where he will hunt for food, and trade cattle,

IMPROVE YOUR MAP SKILLS

It's important as we grow that we learn to understand the world around us. Where are you now physically in relation to where you were yesterday? Today I am at home, whereas yesterday I was at the supermarket. Locate those two locations on the map and explore the space in between in order to gain a sense of distance.

Use your globe or world map for this exercise. Let's consider some famous literary characters and writers and track their whereabouts on the map! Here are some suggestions below, find them if you can!

Seoni, Madhya Pradesh, India — Bagheera, The Jungle Book

Paddington Station, London — Paddington Bear

Cavendish, Prince Edward Island — Anne of Green Gables

Amsterdam, Netherlands — Anne Frank

Let's take this exercise one step further. Pick out one of your favorite storybooks and let's draw a map of the important places in the story. The story can take place anywhere. If it takes place in a castle, draw a map of the rooms in the castle. If it takes place in a small village, draw a map of the neighborhood and the houses that are important to the story. Try to make the map as accurate as you can, but just know it's okay if it's not perfect.

ZIMBABWE

Flame Lily - *Gloriosa superba*

The Flame Lily is not only beautiful, it is used for medicinal purposes as well. Due to overharvesting the flower is now protected under national laws in Zimbabwe.

Papaya Candy (Mapopo)

Zimbabwe has a lengthy growing season where plants such as squash, corn, yams, pumpkins and papaya grow well, but the growing season is followed by a hot and dry period. For this reason, it is important for families in Zimbabwe to preserve food for use later. Mapopo is easy to prepare, stores well, and makes an excellent gift you can share with friends and family.

Matobo National Park hosts thousands of painted rocks and cave paintings that date back many thousands of years. These paintings are significant because they are some of the earliest records we have of society from that period.

Papaya Candy (Mapopo)

1 Peel the papaya and wash well.

2 Slice the papaya into little, bite-sized strips.

3 Place the papaya, mint, grated lemon and sugar over low heat until the sugar dissolves. When the sugar is dissolved it will form a glossy coat over the candy, and won't have any lumps or crystals.

4 Cook for 10 minutes, then set aside for half an hour. Don't touch the candy because it is very hot!

5 Reheat over medium heat until the mixture starts crystallizing.

6 Remove from the heat. Using a spoon and fork, mold into ball or stick shapes. Again, be very careful because the sugar coating can burn you quite easily.

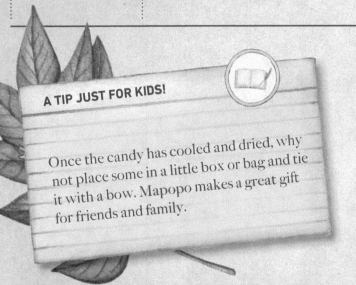

A TIP JUST FOR KIDS!

Once the candy has cooled and dried, why not place some in a little box or bag and tie it with a bow. Mapopo makes a great gift for friends and family.

Ideas for Continued Learning

Watch: Search Youtube for "Muchongoyo" to view the important and distinctive dances performed in Zimbabwe.

Consider: Zimbabwe has sixteen recognized languages spoken in the country. How many languages are commonly spoken in the United States? Is it common for countries to speak more than one language?

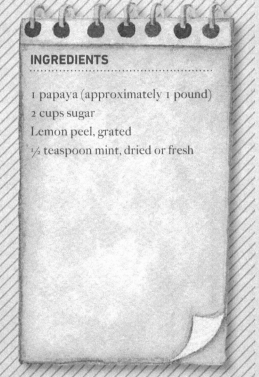

INGREDIENTS

1 papaya (approximately 1 pound)

2 cups sugar

Lemon peel, grated

½ teaspoon mint, dried or fresh

ZIMBABWE

Capital City /	Harare
Nation Language /	English & Shona, etc
Population /	14,862,924
Currency /	RTGS Dollar "Zollar"

In many countries around the world it is common to have an official language that is spoken in government offices and schools, but other languages are spoken by the people in their homes. English and Shona are spoken by 70% of the population in Zimbabwe, but the country actually has 16 official languages.

How the Tortoise Cracked His Shell

Many, many years ago there was a great famine in Africa. The birds of the sky and the animals of the grasslands were very hungry, often going many days without food. The animals helped one another, especially the Go-Away-Birds and the tortoise. They were the best of friends.

One day, the Go-Away-Birds were shrieking with excitement because a great many tender leaves were spotted high in an Acacia tree. They swarmed the tree, feasting in the afternoon sun. However, the tortoise was very sad. "What about me?" he cried. "My family is hungry as well."

The birds wanted to help the tortoise, but they could not think of a solution. "You cannot fly, and these delicious leaves are very high in the tree." They tried plucking some leaves and dropping them to the ground below, but they were swept into the breeze and drifted far away before the tortoise could find them.

The tortoise spotted a feather nestled in the grass and he suddenly had an amazing idea, "Birds, please share with me some of your feathers! If I only had feathers, I could fly as well!" Happy to help, the Go-Away-Birds shared some of their lengthy tail feathers with the tortoise, using sap from the Acacia tree to glue them to his shell.

At first, it was as if a miracle had occurred. The tortoise flew high into the air and circled the Acacia tree, enjoying his newfound freedom. But his freedom was short-lived. One by one, the feathers came undone and soon the tortoise plummeted to the earth below. His smooth shell was cracked into a dozen pieces. The birds helped piece him back together, but the tortoise was never the same. In fact, his descendants carry the same cracked pattern today.

Grey Go-Away-Bird -
Corythaixoides concolor

African Helmeted Turtle -
Pelomedusa subrufa

Getting to Know Zimbabwe

Fill in the missing information on this page. You can find the correct answers in your copy of *The Cultured Chef,* or search online to retrieve the information needed.

Capital City:

Country Population:

Language:

Google Zimbabwe's flag and use as reference to color the drawing below.

ZIMBABWE

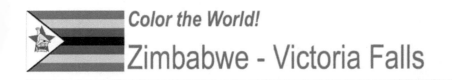

Victoria Falls (Tokaleya Tonga: Mosi-oa-Tunya, "The Smoke that Thunders") rests on the Zambezi River between the countries of Zimbabwe and Zambia. This natural wonder has the distinction of being one of the world's longest and most powerful waterfalls, with mist seen rising into the air from miles away.

GETTING TO KNOW

Influential Africans

Consider learning more about these important figures in African history. Their accomplishments have impacted the way of life not only for African citizens, but the world at large. When reviewing each of these accomplished individuals, please make note of the impact they made on society. Take a moment to reflect upon how your life is improved because of the achievements they made.

Cleopatra VII (70-30 BCE)

Arguably one of the most famous queens in world history, Cleopatra is known for defending Egypt from the Roman Empire, and forming alliances with Julius Caesar and Mark Antony. She was the last of the Egyptian Pharaohs.

Check out these great books

Wangari Maathai: The Woman Who Planted Millions of Trees by Franck Prevot

Nelson Mandela: Long Walk to Freedom by Chris Van W

Cleopatra and Ancient Egypt for Kids by Simonetta Carr

Dr. Christian Barnard (1992-2001)

Dr. Christian Barnard performed the first heart transplant in 1967 in Cape Town, South Africa.

Bertina Lopes (1935-2012)

Bertina was a world-renowned painter and sculptor from Mozambique. Her work was inspired by the poets of her day.

Nelson Mandela (1918-2013)

Nelson Mandela was a civil rights leader who fought against apartheid in South Africa. Apartheid is a system where non-white citizens are separated from the whites, and they do not have equal rights.

Wangari Maathai (1940-2011)

Wangari Maathai was a leading environmentalist and political activist, and she is the first African woman to win the Nobel Prize.

NIGERIA

Nigerian Culture

The culture of Nigeria is very rich and diverse due to the many ethnic groups (over 1100) who live in the country. Indeed, there are over 500 different languages spoken in Nigeria! Spend some time learning about the three main groups called Hausa-Fulani, Igbo, and Yoruba. These groups make up nearly 70% of the population of Nigeria.

Over-ripe Plantain Snack (Dodo Ikire)

It's always fun when a recipe has an interesting history. Dodo Ikire is a very popular snack you can buy from roadside vendors all over Nigeria. It is said that a little old lady didn't have much to eat beside old plantains that were turning black. So instead of throwing them out, she mixed them up with salt and pepper and fried the mixture in oil. She enjoyed the flavor so much, she shared it with her friends and neighbors and instantly became a celebrity because everyone else loved it as well!

Over-ripe Plantain Snack (Dodo Ikire)

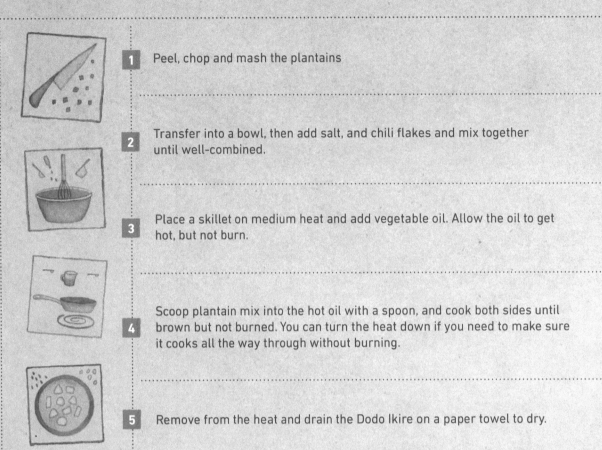

1. Peel, chop and mash the plantains

2. Transfer into a bowl, then add salt, and chili flakes and mix together until well-combined.

3. Place a skillet on medium heat and add vegetable oil. Allow the oil to get hot, but not burn.

4. Scoop plantain mix into the hot oil with a spoon, and cook both sides until brown but not burned. You can turn the heat down if you need to make sure it cooks all the way through without burning.

5. Remove from the heat and drain the Dodo Ikire on a paper towel to dry.

NOTES:

If you don't like spicy foods, maybe you can leave out the chili flakes. Children in Nigeria love this snack, and often remind their parents to bring them back a treat of Dodo Ikire when they are out running errands or returning home from work.

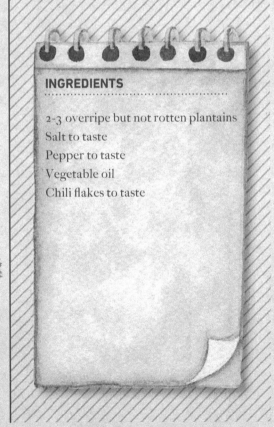

INGREDIENTS

2-3 overripe but not rotten plantains
Salt to taste
Pepper to taste
Vegetable oil
Chili flakes to taste

Ideas for Continued Learning

Compare: Nigeria is often called the "Giant of Africa" because of the large population and the diversity of the ethnic groups. What are some nicknames for other countries in the world? Are these titles official?

Research: Nigerian fashion has some of the most colorful and vibrant patterns in the world. Do a Google image search for "Nigerian Fashion" and see what you find!

NIGERIA

Capital City /	Abuja
Nation Language /	English, etc
Population /	206,102,237
Currency /	Nigerian Naira

A major percentage of Nigerians live in poverty, in fact, it's estimated that nearly 60% of the people don't make enough money to take care of their basic needs. Income inequality, conflict between different groups of people, as well as corrupt local and national government are to blame for Nigeria's extreme poverty.

Why the Moon Waxes and Wanes

There was once an old woman who was very poor. She lived in a mud hut with a dirt floor and a roof thatched with leaves from the bush. Hunger rumbled in her belly almost every day, but she had no one to provide for her. She relied on the generosity of strangers, and what little food she could find on her own.

In these days, the moon visited the earth each day. Spending most of her day resting lazily in the sky, the moon became very fat. She had much meat on her bones and skin on her hide. One day when visiting the earth, the moon felt very sorry for the hungry old woman. "I have enough meat on my body to share," she offered the woman. What a wonderful arrangement! The hungry old woman reached up to the moon and carved off a slice for her meal.

Each day, the moon visited the woman and took her share of food. But each day, the moon grew thinner and thinner until the people of the village became worried. The moon no longer provided enough light to see at night. So the next night, when the moon came down to earth, the villagers made lots of noise and scared the woman away before she could collect the moon's meat. They scared the moon so much so, she stopped coming to earth any longer. However, to this day, the moon still waxes and wanes. Perhaps the little old woman found another way to help herself to the moon's abundant meat.

Getting to Know Nigeria

Fill in the missing information on this page. You can find the correct answers in your copy of *The Cultured Chef,* or search online to retrieve the information needed.

Capital City:

Country Population:

Language:

Google Nigeria's flag and use as reference to color the drawing below.

NIGERIA

It is estimated that over fifty percent of the Nigerian population is Muslim. Muslim mosques can be seen throughout the country.

A Nigerian woman wearing a hijab. A hijab is a veil worn by some Muslim women when they are in public, outside their immediate family.

Umbrella Thorn Acacia - *Vachellia tortilis*

The Kingdom of Losetho

Did you know that South Africa hosts a country within a country? There is a small nation called Lesotho nestled on the steep slopes of the Great Escarpment, a mountainous area that stretches across South Africa. South Africa completely surrounds the tiny kingdom.

Impala - *Aepyceros melampus*

Southeast African Cheetah - *Acinonyx jubatus jubatus*

South Africa

∽ Bobotie ∽

The further you dig into the history of certain dishes around the world, the more you realize it's very difficult to find a dish that is uniquely from one place. Bobotie has a very long history dating back to Indonesia. Interestingly, the Romans included a recipe in a popular cookbook written over 1,100 years ago. But it was the Dutch who introduced the dish in South Africa where it became very popular. To South Africans, Bobotie is as common as eating a casserole in the US.

South Africa is the southernmost nation in Africa, stretching across the entire tip of the continent. As one of the most diverse countries in the world, South Africa is often labeled as the "Rainbow Nation" due to the variety of ethnic groups and languages.

South Africa was colonized by the Dutch and British for many years. The country struggled due to an unjust system of laws that required non-white citizens to live separately from whites, stripping them of their rights. Known as Apartheid, this system continued until 1994 when the first Black head of state was elected in South Africa.

Bay Laurel - Laurus nobilis

The Ship Graveyard

Over the years there have been more than 2000 shipwrecks off the South African coast due to dangerous conditions and rugged coastline. In an attempt to prevents these shipwrecks, many lighthouses have been constructed along the South African coastline.

Bobotie

1 Preheat the oven to 350 degrees. Combine the bread and milk in a small bowl, and let the bread soak for 10 minutes.

2 In a heavy saucepan melt the butter and oil; stir in the onions and cook slowly until they are soft. Add the curry, sugar, salt and pepper, and stir for about 30 seconds. Next, stir in the lamb and saute until well browned. Add the lemon juice, bring the mixture to a boil and remove from heat.

3 Drain the bread, and squeeze to dry it completely, reserving the drained milk.

4 Add the bread, one of the eggs and the apple to the lamb. Beat the mixture with a wooden spoon until the ingredients are well blended. Taste for seasoning. Pack the mixture loosely into an ovenproof baking dish, and tuck the bay leaves underneath.

5 Whisk the remaining eggs with the reserved milk until it becomes frothy. Pour this mixture evenly over the meat, and bake in the middle rack of the oven for 30 minutes, until the surface has browned and is firm. Serve directly from the pan.

A TIP JUST FOR KIDS!

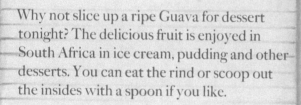

Why not slice up a ripe Guava for dessert tonight? The delicious fruit is enjoyed in South Africa in ice cream, pudding and other desserts. You can eat the rind or scoop out the insides with a spoon if you like.

Ideas for Continued Learning

Research: Do a Google image search for "Bo-Kaap," a colorful neighborhood with cobblestone streets in Cape Town, South Africa. Use Google Maps to determine how many miles it is from Bo-Kaap to your house!

Watch: Search Youtube for "Kgati" a traditional South African rope skipping and jumping game. Maybe you can try this game with your friends.

Discover: What is colonization? South Africa was colonized by the Dutch and British. Learn what this means, and find what other colonies exist in the world.

INGREDIENTS

1 slice white bread

1 cup milk

1 tablespoon unsalted butter

2 tablespoons vegetable oil

1 ½ cups finely chopped onion

2 tablespoons curry powder

1 tablespoon brown sugar

2 pounds ground lean lamb or pork

¼ cup lemon juice

3 eggs

1 Granny Smith apple, peeled and finely grated

4 small bay leaves

SOUTH AFRICA

Capital City / Pretoria (executive)

Language / English, Afrikaans, Zulu, etc

Population / 57,725,600

Currency / South African Rand

A set of limestone caves called Sterkfontein were discovered near Johannesburg, a site where archeologists have found human fossils dating back more than two million years! Because of the age of these discoveries, archeologists and scientists call this region "The cradle of humankind."

Nelson Mandela

Nelson Mandela (1918-2013) was a civil rights leader who later became the first Black president of South Africa. He is celebrated because he spent the majority of his life fighting against an unfair system called apartheid. Many people suffered under this system where non-white citizens were segregated from whites. There were laws set in place that made it illegal for whites and non-whites to live or work together. In fact, special permission was required by many to even travel through so-called "white areas" in South Africa.

Mandela worked with the African National Congress to try to end apartheid, and in doing so he was arrested and imprisoned for 27 years. During this time he refused to change his way of thinking, so the government chose not to release him. He became a national symbol of the people who were against apartheid.

Finally released from prison in 1990, Mandela went on to win the Nobel Peace Prize and become the president of South Africa. By the time of his death, he had become known as the "father of the nation" of South Africa. That's quite an achievement!

Getting to Know South Africa

Fill in the missing information on this page. You can find the correct answers in your copy of *The Cultured Chef,* or search online to retrieve the information needed.

Capital City:

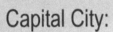

Country Population:

Languages:

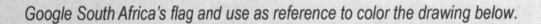

Google South Africa's flag and use as reference to color the drawing below.

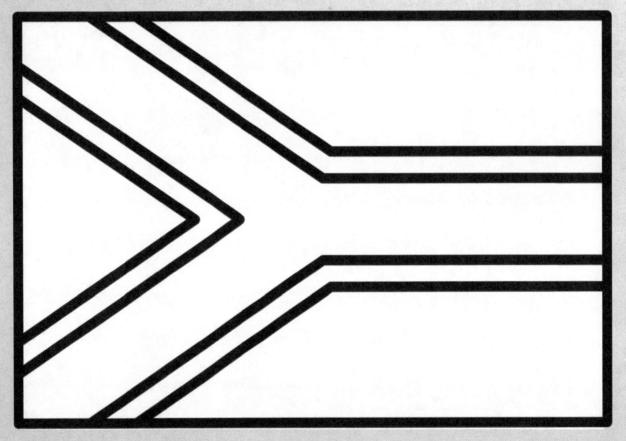

SOUTH AFRICA

South Africa - The Baobab Tree

The Baobab tree is a very unique species that can live for many, many years. Some of the Baobab have been discovered to be over 2400 years old. The fruit weighs around 3 lbs, and has a citris flavor.

The Flora and Fauna of Africa

The continent of Africa borders the Mediterranean Sea, the Atlantic Ocean, the Indian Ocean, and passes through the equator as well. The continent covers more than 12 million square miles making it the second largest continent in terms of size, and second largest in terms of population. Africa is one of the most diverse places on the planet with an immense variety of terrain, wildlife, and climates.

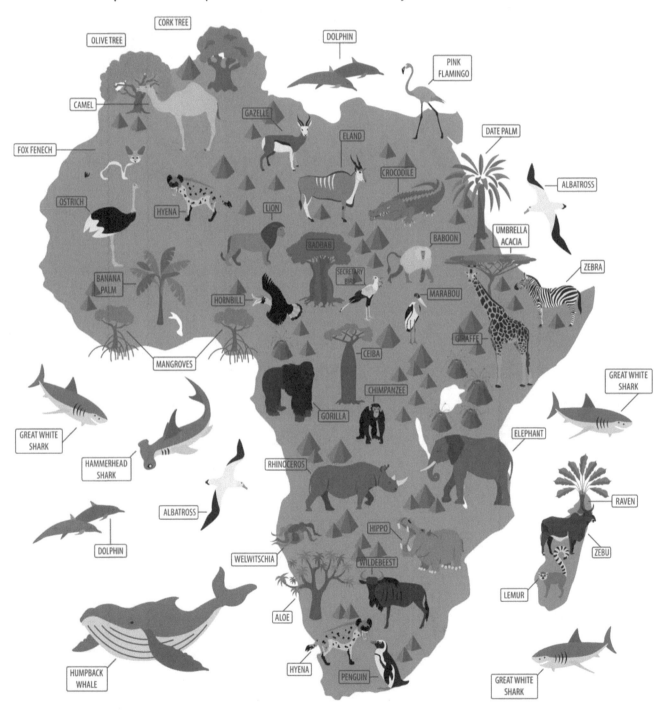

Animals
of Africa

There is a lot to consider when learning about animals of the world. Different animals are suited to different climates, and have particular tastes when it comes to the food they need to survive. A penguin won't feel very much at home on the beach in Miami, Florida, would it?

Select an animal from the previous page about Africa and write a short report below. Where does the animal live? What does the animal like to eat? Are there any other facts about this animal you find interesting?

Use the space below to write down interesting facts about the animal you have chosen.

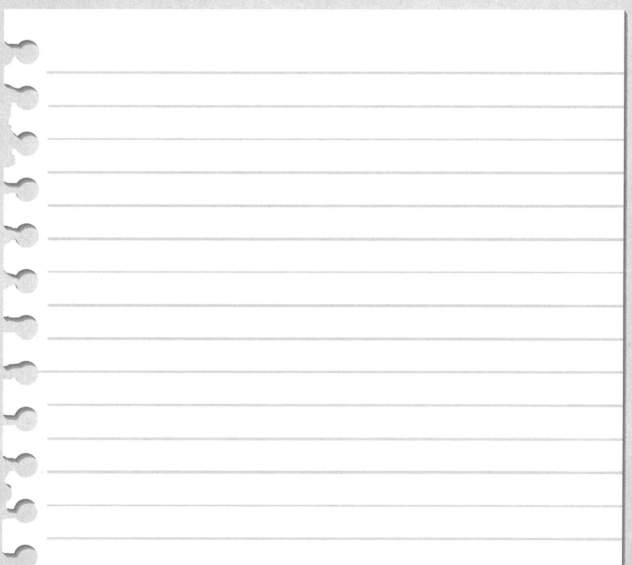

AFRICA

"Aim for the highest cloud so that if you miss it, you will hit a lofty mountain."

Māori Proverb, Author Unknown

OCEANIA

N
W E
S

NEW ZEALAND - AUSTRALIA

New Zealand

Anna Pavlova was a Russian ballerina with a very successful career in the early 1900s. She was known for her delicate beauty and grace and for being one of the earliest ballerinas to achieve worldwide fame. Can you believe she performed her most famous role in The Dying Swan over 4,000 times during her lifetime? Pavlova was so famous that in 1926 when she toured New Zealand and Australia, everyone wanted a chance to see her perform.

A National Dish

Legend has it that a chef in Wellington, New Zealand was so inspired by her performance, he created a light and airy meringue dessert named in her honor. The dessert has been plagued with controversy ever since. Both Australia and New Zealand claim Pavlova as their "national dish" and have argued about it for decades. While the truth may never be known, some of the earliest references to the dessert suggest the chef in New Zealand was the creator of the delicious treat.

Strawberry - *Fragaria X ananassa*

Kowhai - *Sophora microphylla*

North Island Brown Kiwi: *Apteryx mantelli* - The kiwi is a large, flightless bird about the size of a chicken, with a characteristic long bill. The bird is often seen as a symbol for New Zealand, appearing on military badges, postage stamps and currency. With around 35,000 birds living, the North Island Brown Kiwi is the most common kiwi found in New Zealand. However, because their numbers have decreased greatly in the last 100 years, it is now listed as an endangered species.

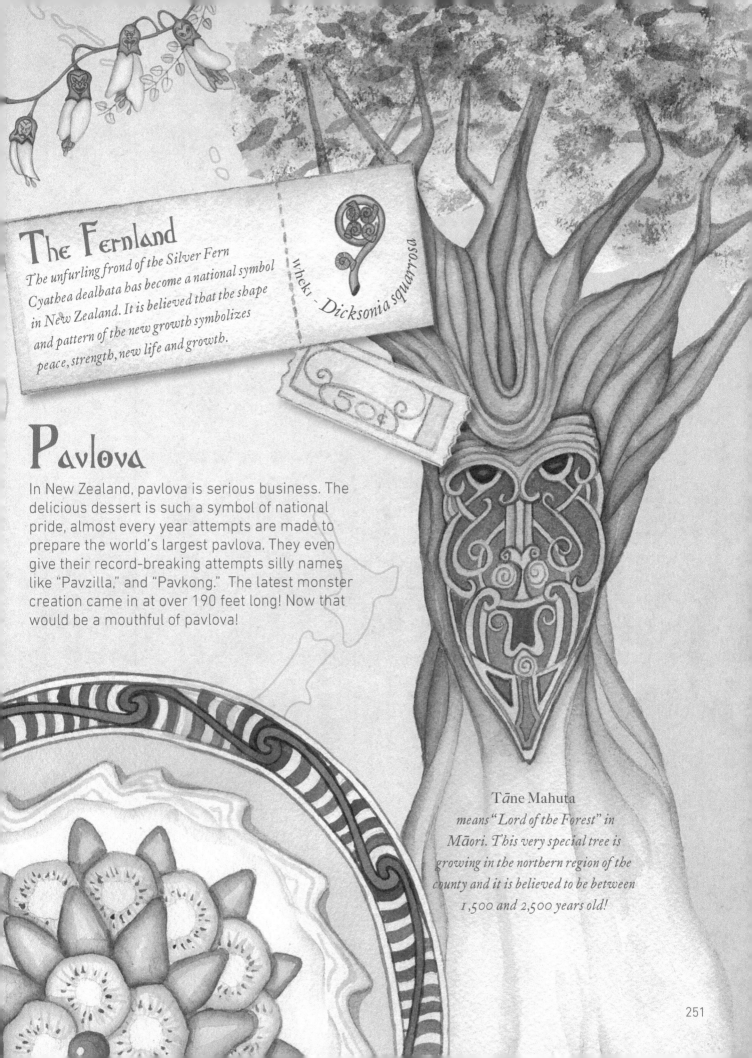

The Fernland

The unfurling frond of the Silver Fern Cyathea dealbata has become a national symbol in New Zealand. It is believed that the shape and pattern of the new growth symbolizes peace, strength, new life and growth.

wheki - Dicksonia squarrosa

Pavlova

In New Zealand, pavlova is serious business. The delicious dessert is such a symbol of national pride, almost every year attempts are made to prepare the world's largest pavlova. They even give their record-breaking attempts silly names like "Pavzilla," and "Pavkong." The latest monster creation came in at over 190 feet long! Now that would be a mouthful of pavlova!

Tāne Mahuta means "Lord of the Forest" in Māori. This very special tree is growing in the northern region of the county and it is believed to be between 1,500 and 2,500 years old!

251

Pavlova

1 Place rack in the middle of the oven and preheat oven to 300 degrees Fahrenheit. Line a baking sheet with parchment paper and draw a 9-inch circle in the center. Turn the paper over, pencil marks facing down.

2 In a large bowl, beat the egg whites until soft peaks form. Continue beating, adding 1 tablespoon of sugar at a time until all of the sugar is incorporated and the mixture becomes thick and glossy. Sprinkle in vanilla extract, lemon juice and cornstarch and fold the ingredients into mixture.

3 With a spatula, transfer mixture into the center of the circle on the parchment paper. From the center, spread the mixture evenly toward the outside edge. Be sure to create a slight depression in the center, building up the edges. This ensures that when it's time to heap on the whipping cream none of it will slide off!

4 Bake for 1 hour, turn off the oven and allow to cool completely inside the oven. Note: The meringue should be white. Check while it is baking and if you see it turning tan or beginning to crack, reduce the temperature by 25 degrees.

5 In a small bowl, beat cream until it begins to form stiff peaks, then set it aside. Prepare the meringue by removing the paper and placing on a dessert plate. Spread whipping cream on top of the dessert in the depression you formed before baking. Top with slices of kiwi and strawberry in any pattern you like.

A TIP JUST FOR KIDS!

"Pavlova is best served immediately upon placing the fruit and whipped cream. Slice the dessert with a serrated knife. If there are any leftovers, store in an air-tight container."

Ideas for Continued Learning

Watch: The film series The Lord of the Rings was famously filmed in New Zealand. Have you seen any of the films? If you haven't, it's ok. The natural landscape of New Zealand is very beautiful. Search Youtube for "Nature of New Zealand" for videos showcasing the natural beauty.

INGREDIENTS

4 egg whites
1 1/4 cups white sugar
2 teaspoons cornstarch
1 teaspoon vanilla extract
1 teaspoon lemon juice
1 cup sliced fruit (kiwifruit, strawberries)
1 cup lightly sweetened whipped cream

NEW ZEALAND

Capital City / Wellington

Nation Language / English

Population / 4,365,113

Currency / New Zealand Dollar

New Zealand *is the product of volcanic activity as massive undersea eruptions created both the North and South Islands over many years. The island nation has more than 50 volcanoes, some of which are still active.*

The Golden Kawhai – A Folk Tale of the Maori People

Sophora microphylla, known as Kōwhai (meaning "yellow" in Māori) is a small tree with bright yellow flowers that is commonly found in most parts of New Zealand. This story explains how the tree came to be.

Many years ago, before the Europeans came to New Zealand, a young couple sat beneath a tree bare of leaves or flowers. It was clear the two were in love – they had spent every moment together for weeks. And, now it was time for the young man to ask the young lady for her hand in marriage. But, her answer surprised him.

"I can only marry a man who can perform great and unexplained miracles," she said. The young man was stunned for a moment. "You shall see what I can do," he said simply. With no motion at all, he spoke ancient and mysterious words aloud. For a second the two stared at one another, saying nothing. Then with a wink of his eye, he stood to his feet and commanded, "Great dormant tree, I command you to flower before our eyes!" With that, the tree erupted into a great, wild mass of golden flowers. The young girl had no choice but to say yes.

The Maori People

The Māori are the indigenous, or native, people of New Zealand. Over 1,250 years ago, Polynesian explorers travelled the South Pacific in giant canoes and when they happened across the shores of New Zealand decided to stay. In 1769, when the British explorer Captain James Cook first visited New Zealand, he estimated there were over 150,000 Māori people living in the region.

The Māori people have strong cultural and religious beliefs involving nature. They believe there are many different gods who are represented by the sky, the earth, flowers, forests and even the forces of nature. They celebrate and give thanks to their gods through song and dance, and special masks and carvings.

Getting to Know New Zealand

Fill in the missing information on this page. You can find the correct answers in your copy of *The Cultured Chef,* or search online to retrieve the information needed.

Capital City:

Country Population:

Languages:

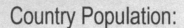

Google New Zealand's flag and use as reference to color the drawing below.

Color the World!

New Zealand - Māori Culture

The Māori are the indigenous, or native, people of New Zealand. Over 1,250 years ago, Polynesian explorers traveled the South Pacific in giant canoes and when they happened across the shores of New Zealand decided to stay.

ANIMALS OF THE WORLD

Scientists who study animals are called zoologists. Throughout history, they have recorded more than 20,000 species of fish, 6,000 species of reptiles, 9,000 birds, 1,000 amphibians, and over 15,000 species of mammals! The list of animals that share our planet with us is incredible! How many different species of animals can you think of?

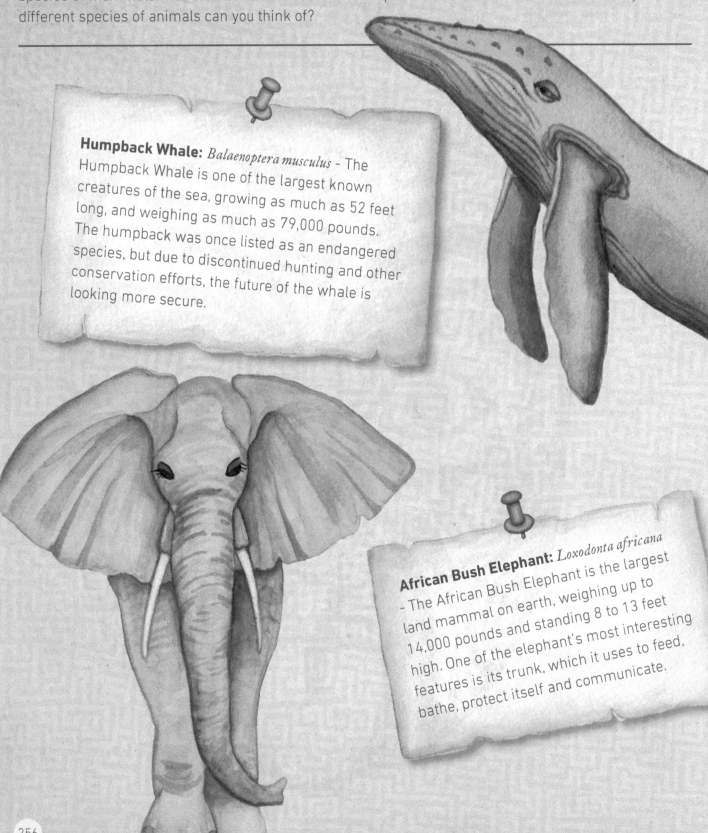

Humpback Whale: *Balaenoptera musculus* – The Humpback Whale is one of the largest known creatures of the sea, growing as much as 52 feet long, and weighing as much as 79,000 pounds. The humpback was once listed as an endangered species, but due to discontinued hunting and other conservation efforts, the future of the whale is looking more secure.

African Bush Elephant: *Loxodonta africana* – The African Bush Elephant is the largest land mammal on earth, weighing up to 14,000 pounds and standing 8 to 13 feet high. One of the elephant's most interesting features is its trunk, which it uses to feed, bathe, protect itself and communicate.

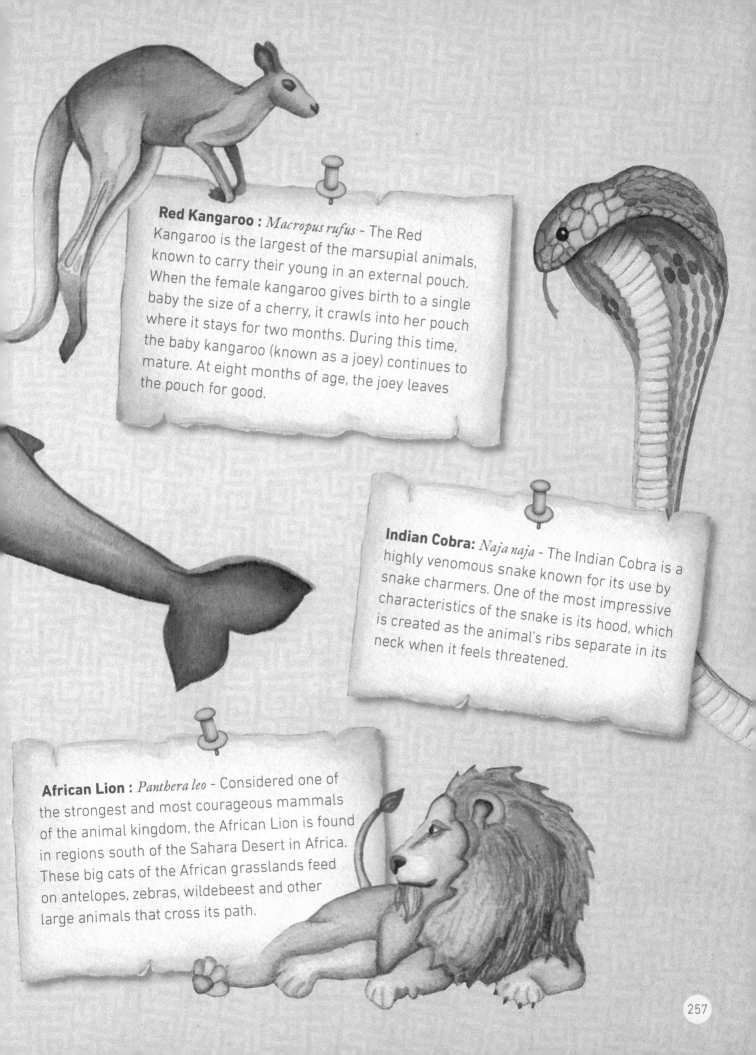

Red Kangaroo : *Macropus rufus* – The Red Kangaroo is the largest of the marsupial animals, known to carry their young in an external pouch. When the female kangaroo gives birth to a single baby the size of a cherry, it crawls into her pouch where it stays for two months. During this time, the baby kangaroo (known as a joey) continues to mature. At eight months of age, the joey leaves the pouch for good.

Indian Cobra: *Naja naja* – The Indian Cobra is a highly venomous snake known for its use by snake charmers. One of the most impressive characteristics of the snake is its hood, which is created as the animal's ribs separate in its neck when it feels threatened.

African Lion : *Panthera leo* – Considered one of the strongest and most courageous mammals of the animal kingdom, the African Lion is found in regions south of the Sahara Desert in Africa. These big cats of the African grasslands feed on antelopes, zebras, wildebeest and other large animals that cross its path.

Australia is the only country in the world that covers an entire continent. While it's roughly the same size as the United States in terms of land mass, there is only a population of 25,000,000 people. The majority of the population in Australia lives in the coastal areas of the southwest and southeast portion of the country.

The Outback

A vast portion of the continent is wide open space known as the outback. While it may seem fun to roam around in this wide open space, keep in mind that a large portion of the area is very hot and dry, and perhaps a little dangerous given the distance from major population centers. Much of the land is left to nature, with the exception of some farming and grazing.

Eastern Grey Kangaroo - *Macropus giganteus*

New South Wales Waratah - *Telopea speciosissima*

Australia

Great Barrier Reef

Located in the Coral Sea off the Queensland coast, the Great Barrier Reef is the world's largest network of coral reef stretching over 1,400 miles! This special ecosystem hosts a wide variety of plant and animal species, many of which are endangered. Recently, large portions of the reef are dying off due to rising ocean temperatures and pollution.

Meat Pies

Meat pies are often referred to as Australia's national dish. According to some sources, it's estimated that a majority of Australians eat 15 meat pies a year! It makes sense since the dish can be eaten as a snack at a football game, or a quick lunch between classes. There's even a national competition held annually to identify the best manufacturer of pies.

If you don't eat meat, don't worry. These pies can be made as cheese or vegetarian options as well.

Southern Blue Gum - Eucalyptus globulusgiganteus

Meat Pies

1 Preheat oven to 400 degrees F (200 degrees C). Grease a 12-cup muffin tin.

2 Heat a large skillet over medium-high heat. Cook and stir ground beef and onion in the hot skillet until meat is browned and crumbly, 5 to 7 minutes. Drain fat. Add 3/4 cup chicken broth, ketchup, Worcestershire sauce, oregano, and black pepper. Bring to a boil, reduce heat, and simmer about 10 minutes.

3 Mix remaining 1/4 cup chicken broth and cornstarch together in a bowl to form a paste; stir into meat mixture. Cook until thickened, about 5 minutes more. Remove from heat.

4 Use a 4-inch biscuit cutter to cut the pie crusts into 12 circles. Line each muffin cup with a circle, pressing into the bottom and sides. Fill each with the meat mixture. Use a 3-inch biscuit cutter to cut puff pastry dough into 12 circles. Top each filled muffin cup with with a circle and seal edges together. Brush pastry tops with beaten egg. Bake in the preheated oven until crusts are brown and flaky, 15 to 20 minutes. Cool in pan before removing pies, about 10 minutes.

A TIP JUST FOR KIDS!

Vegemite is one of the most iconic Australian food products that has gained attention all over the world. If you can get your hands on a bottle, you should definitely give it a try. It's made from vegetable paste, yeast extract and various spices.

Ideas for Continued Learning

Research: The history and the culture of the Aboriginal people of Australia deserves more study. Start with a Google image search for "Anangu," a large indigenous population. Click on any photos that seem interesting to you and read what you can about the photo.

Discover: The flora and fauna (plant and animal life) in Australia is very unique. Learn what plants and animals are native to Australia.

Listen: No study of Australia is complete without listening to "Traditional Didgeridoo Rhythms." See what you can find on Youtube.

INGREDIENTS

1 pound ground beef

1 onion, chopped

1 cup chicken broth, divided

1/4 cup ketchup

2 teaspoons Worcestershire sauce

1/2 teaspoon dried oregano

1/2 teaspoon salt

1/4 cup cornstarch

1/4 cup cold water

1 (15 ounce) package refrigerated pie crusts for a double-crust pie

1 sheet frozen puff pastry, thawed

1 egg, beaten

AUSTRALIA

Capital City / Canberra	
Nation Language / English	
Population / 25,497,200	
Currency / Australian Dollar	

The first people to live in Australia, the indigenous population, are known as Aboriginal people. The Aboriginal people make up about 2% of Australia's population, and it is believed they are direct descendants of Africans dating back more than 75,000 years. Aboriginal culture is rich and diverse, and deserves to be studied in more detail.

Why the Topknot Pigeons Feed Together

This story comes from the Ualarai culture, an indigenous people who originated from the New South Wales area of Australia. The elders would use this story to explain why the birds traveled and fed in flocks, rather than singly. Tales like this are often told to explain why things are the way they are.

Young Goolahwilleel used to go hunting every day, leaving his mother and sisters anticipating the kangaroo or emu he would return with. Their mouths watered at the thought of the juicy meat roasting over the fire at night. However, Goolahwilleel always fell short! The sisters would hear his call, "Prepare the fire, I've caught our dinner!" But he would always return empty handed.

Night after night, his mother and sisters would ask, "Did you bring us anything home?" He laughed and smiled, "Tomorrow, I promise. I will bring you a kangaroo."

Indeed, every day when Goolahwilleel went out in search of food, he instead spent his time collecting wattle-gum he used to model a kangaroo, complete with ears, eyes and a great big tail! So that night he called for his sisters to ready the fire. He returned with the wattle-gum kangaroo, fashioned by his own hands, and his family nearly lost their minds! "What is this madness?" the poor, hungry sisters asked.

From that day forward, Goolahwilleel always went hunting with a group because his mother and sisters didn't trust him to bring an emu or kangaroo home otherwise.

Getting to Know Australia

Fill in the missing information on this page. You can find the correct answers in your copy of *The Cultured Chef,* or search online to retrieve the information needed.

Capital City:

Country Population:

Languages:

Google Australia's flag and use as reference to color the drawing below.

AUSTRALIA

Australia - The Sydney Opera House

The Sydney Opera House is an iconic symbol of Australia that was opened to the public in 1973. The building represents a ship at full sail set against the backdrop of the harbor.

The Flora and Fauna of Australia

Australia has the distinction of being the only country in the world that covers an entire continent. It is also one of the largest countries on Earth. Though the continent is rich in natural resources and has lots of fertile land suitable for crop production, more than one-third of Australia is desert. Because Australia is so far removed from other land masses in the world, there are many plant and animal species that are not found anywhere else.

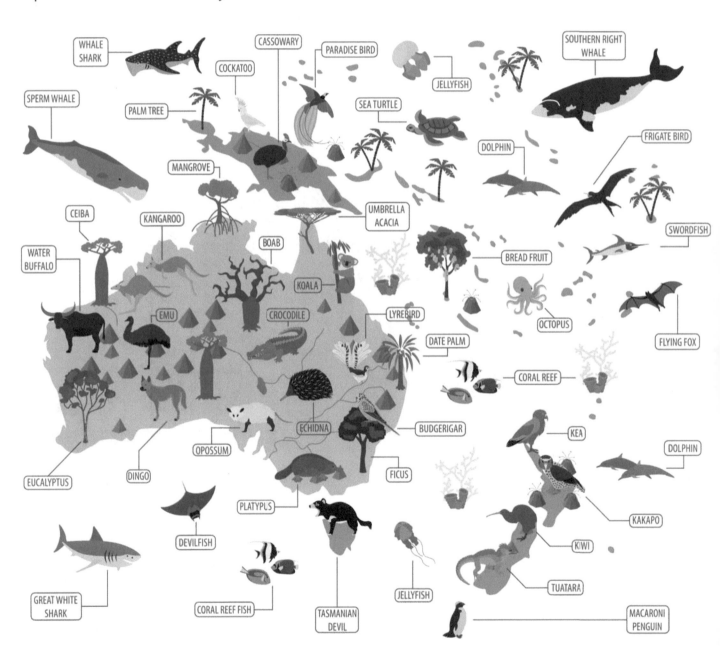

Animals
of Australia

There is a lot to consider when learning about animals of the world. Different animals are suited to different climates, and have particular tastes when it comes to the food they need to survive. A penguin won't feel very much at home on the beach in Miami, Florida, would it?

Select an animal from the previous page about Australia and write a short report below. Where does the animal live? What does the animal like to eat? Are there any other facts about this animal you find interesting?

Use the space below to write down interesting facts about the animal you have chosen.

AUSTRALIA

The Flora and Fauna of Antarctica

Antarctica is surrounded by the Southern Ocean. The continent is larger than Europe and almost nearly double the size of Australia. The majority of the continent is covered in ice over a mile thick! Surprisingly, because the continent experiences very little rain, Antarctica is considered a desert. There are not many species of animals living in this region, with the exception of whales, seals and penguins. Check out the chart below and research your favorites!

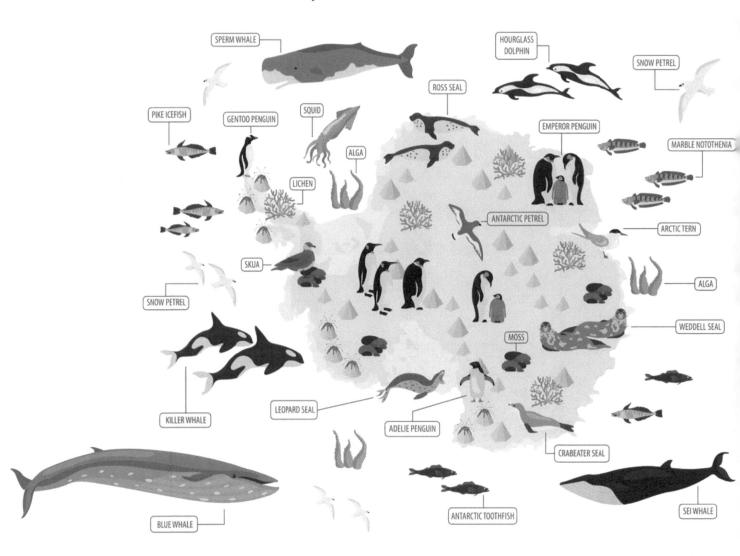

Animals
of Antarctica

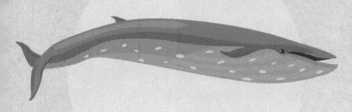

There is a lot to consider when learning about animals of the world. Different animals are suited to different climates, and have particular tastes when it comes to the food they need to survive. A penguin won't feel very much at home on the beach in Miami, Florida, would it?

Select an animals from the previous page about Antarctica and write a short report below. Where does the animal live? What does the animal like to eat? Are there any other facts about this animal you find interesting?

Use the space below to write down interesting facts about the animal you have chosen.

HOW TO INCORPORATE
THIS BOOK INTO THE CLASSROOM

This is more than a list of lesson plans; it is a springboard for your own unique style of teaching based on the students you have in your classroom this year. All the activities and ideas are aligned with the Common Core State Standards for English Language Arts using both literary and informational text.

The National Council of Teachers of English believes that literacy growth begins before children enter school as they experience and experiment with literacy activities: reading and writing and associating spoken words with their graphic representations.

This book also supports the NCTE Standards for English Language Arts:

- Read texts to acquire new information.
- Apply a wide range of strategies to comprehend, interpret and appreciate texts.
- Conduct research on interests by generating ideas and questions, and gather, evaluate, and synthesize data from a variety of sources.
- Read texts to build an understanding of oneself and the world's cultures.
- Develop an understanding of and respect for diversity in language use, patterns and dialects across cultures, ethnic groups, geographic regions and social roles.

Go to CulturedChef.com for an extensive collection of educator resources.

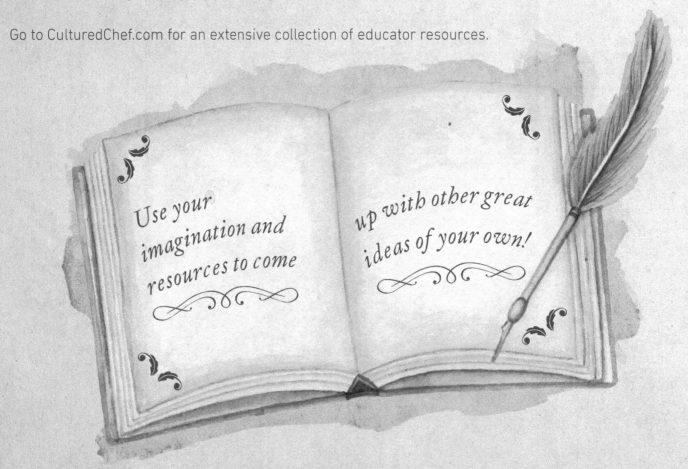

Use your imagination and resources to come up with other great ideas of your own!

Grades K-2

Focus Activity:
Have students create a "T Chart" listing their favorite foods on one side and foods they might not like as well on the other. Help them locate some of their favorites in the ingredients lists from the recipes. This could be the basis for many different types of activities or lessons across the curriculum. For social studies, you could show familiar cross-cultural characteristics. In reading, you could create a comprehension lesson using compare/contrast skills. For math, a graphing activity could focus on "which cultures use how many of your favorite ingredients?"

Other Ideas:
— Use this resource as a picture book. Read aloud the vignettes from each country to encourage curiosity about different cultures around the world.

— Use the rich visual format of this book to engage children in recognizing colors, shapes, numbers, amounts, letters, letter sounds and words.

Grade 3

Focus Activity:
To help students rethink text in a different genre, create or locate a Found Poetry activity where they can spend some time locating words or phrases from a section of The Cultured Chef. Perhaps they will create a poem around gardening, art or music. Or they might choose any of the represented cultures. After students choose words and phrases that appeal to them, they can create a line for a class poem to which everyone contributes.

Other Ideas:
— After students choose one of the cultures represented in the book, have them create a KWL chart to guide their thinking and learning. Students can research the country they chose and fill out the chart as they go. If you want to encourage students to continue their learning and becoming experts, they could write reports, create presentations, etc.

— In some school districts across the nation, third graders participate in a "Culture Fair." For this project, they begin researching the culture of their heritage at the beginning of the year, adding to their knowledge as time goes on. In the spring, the students convene in an agreed upon area to display their presentations of learning.

HOW TO INCORPORATE
THIS BOOK INTO THE CLASSROOM

Grade 4

Focus Activity:

Incorporate the gardening pages by having students learn about helpful and harmful insects. In groups, students could brainstorm short lists of bugs they've seen in vegetable or flower beds. Then they could each choose an insect for research to determine what the different functions of these bugs are in gardens and how they affect plants and other aspects of a "growing habitat." Expert group share-out presentations could include posters, PowerPoint presentations or other creative visuals.

Other Ideas:

— The above activity could be a springboard to other science topics such as heredity, adaptation, behaviors and structure; it integrates more than one discipline (reading, writing, science, technology and/or art) into the activity.

— A focus on science could include many geography and ecosystems activities with emphasis on climates, terrains and growing seasons. A focus question for many of these activities could be, "How does the geography of a place affect the culture of that region?"

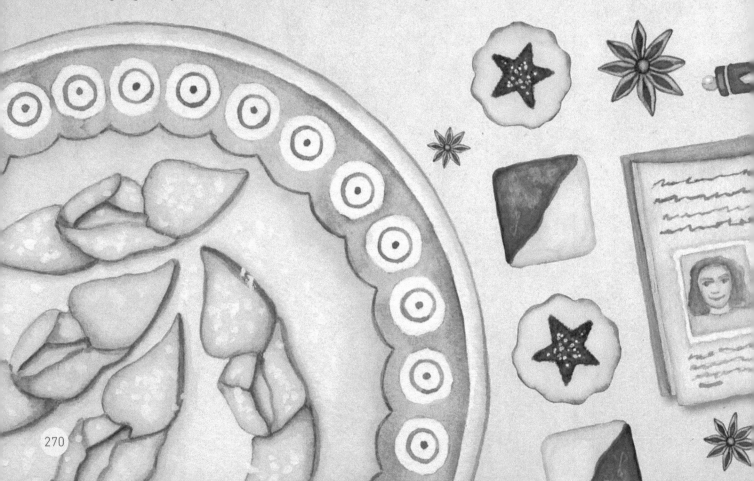

Focus Activity:

Use this book to help students understand units of measure. Have students choose recipes in the book that sound interesting and delicious to them. Ask them to write down how many cups, for example, of an ingredient is needed. Then ask them to convert that measurement to pints or fluid ounces. You can extend this activity by asking students to find equivalencies in many different units of measure.

Bonus: Because most countries use a different system of measurement, have students convert their standard measurements to metric.

Other Ideas:

— Use the "How Much Will It Cost?" activity on page 75 as a classroom math project. Have students create the recipe and enjoy it in class afterward.

— Recipes are a natural for teaching and understanding fractions. Use those found in this book to connect your math lessons to social studies or science content you may also be teaching.

— Write word problems based on the recipes and/or vignettes in the book.

MULTICULTURAL READING LIST

PreK

- Grandmother's Nursery Rhymes by Nelly Palacio Jaramilo
- Margaret and Margarita by Lynn Reiser
- I Love My Hair by Natasha Tarpley
- Baby Rattlesnake by Te Ata
- We're Roaming in the Rainforest by Laurie Krebs
- How Many Seeds in a Pumpkin? By Margaret McNamara

Primary

- Drumbeat... Heartbeat: A Celebration of the Powwow by Susan Braine
- Halmoni and the Picnic by Sook Nyul Choi
- From the Bellybutton of the Moon: and Other Summer Poems by Francisco X. Alarcon
- The People Could Fly: American Black Folktales by Virginia Hamilton
- Senorita Gordita by Helen Ketteman
- The Eclipse by Nicholas Beatty
- Horse Songs: The Naadam of Mongolia by Ted and Betsy Lewin
- Martina the Beautiful Cockroach: A Cuban Folktale by Carmen Agra Deedy
- When Turtle Grew Feathers: A Tale from the Choctaw Nation by Tim Tingle

Intermediate

- Baseball Saved Us by Ken Mochizuki
- John Henry by Julius Lester
- Tar Beach by Faith Ringgold
- Bud, Not Buddy by Christopher Paul Curtis
- The Birchbark House by Louise Erdrich
- Esperanza Rising by Pam Munoz Ryan
- The Rainbow People by Laurence Yep
- The Night the Animals Danced by Nicholas Beatty
- Quilted Landscape: Conversations with Young Immigrants by Yale Strom
- I Lay My Stitches Down: Poems of American Slavery by Cynthia Grady
- Same Sun Here by Silas House and Neela Vaswani
- The Boy Who Harnessed the Wind by William Kawamba and Bryan Mealer

Middle School

- Roll of Thunder, Hear My Cry by Mildred D. Taylor
- The Friends by Kazumi Yumoto
- Bless Me, Ultima by Rudolfo A. Anaya
- Copper Sun by Sharon Draper
- All the Broken Pieces by Ann E. Burg
- Mare's War by Tanita S. Davis
- Alligator Bayou by Donna Jo Napoli
- Dragonwings by Laurence Yep

High School

- Bitter Melon by Cara Chow
- The House on Mango Street by Sandra Cisneros
- Code Talker by Joseph Bruchac
- Does My Head Look Big In This? by Randa Abdel-Fattah
- The Orange Houses by Paul Griffin
- The Absolutely True Diary of a Part-time Indian by Sherman Alexie
- Black, White, Other by Joan Steinau Lester
- Color of the Sea by John Hamamura

- Bitter Melon by Cara Chow
- The Eclipse by Nicholas Beatty
- Baby Rattlesnake by Te Atta

- Tar Beach by Faith Ringgold

- Color of the Sea by John Hamamura

SKILL LEVELS

In other countries, children do a lot of food preparation and cooking. Generally, this is because families have to share a tremendous workload. Often domestic chores will be left to kids while parents work in the fields, herd animals or even leave the home to work in another location. All children are capable and can be taught many skills at an early age. Here are some skills and tasks that young cooks and growing cooks can master:

2 Year Olds

Children want to help at a very early age. When you work with your child in the kitchen, safety is key. Very small children can stay close to you, watch you cook and help in the following ways:
• Wash their hands
• Wipe off counter tops
• Wash fruits and veggies (you can teach them the names of the foods while they wash.)
• Stir batter or other ingredients in bowls
• Mash ingredients with forks or mashers

3-5 Year Olds

Children have widely varied ability levels at these ages. You will be the best judge of which skills your child should try to master first.
• Knead and shape dough
• Grease pans
• Using cookie cutters
• Open packages
• Peel oranges or hard-cooked eggs
• Tear herbs, lettuces, and other leafy veggies
• Spreading peanut butter, butter, and other spreads on bread or dough

5-7 Year Olds

As children get a little older, the skills they are able to master become a little more complex. Always remember to keep an eye on your kiddos in the kitchen, especially when they begin using cutting utensils.
• Measure ingredients
• Cut soft foods with a blunt or plastic knife
• Set the table
• Snip herbs with "school" scissors
• Garnish food
• Making pie crusts and scones by rubbing in flour and butter using fingertips
• Beat eggs or batters with a whisk

8-10 Year Olds

These are the ages where you will begin to let children work with a little more independence. Continue to monitor their safety, giving pointers and tips where needed. Let them problem-solve and plan more at this age to encourage engagement.

• Help plan the meal
• Find ingredients in cupboards, fridge, or spice rack
• Open cans
• Use a peeler, garlic press, and hand grater
• Boil eggs
• Use the microwave, with supervision
• Begin using knives, with supervision
• Make a salad

11-12 Year Olds

At this age, children tend to rush through activities they have done before. Your child may feel s/he is completely capable of all kitchen work at this stage, but when introducing new skills and equipment, continue to provide careful supervision.

• Use a microwave oven
• Prepare simple recipes with few ingredients
• Roast vegetables
• Melt chocolate in the microwave
• Use a hand mixer
• Steam rice
• Begin using the stove and oven, with supervision
• Fry eggs
• Grill sandwiches
• Cook pancakes
• Make soup

13-16 Year Olds

Older cooks like to experiment with recipes and presentation. Allow lots of creativity — while reminding them not to vary the recipes too much — and continue to use safe habits.

• Prepare recipes with multiple ingredients
• Prepare recipes independently
• Safely use kitchen appliances
• Marinate foods
• Bake yeast doughs and pastries

MEASUREMENT & SUBSTITUTION GUIDE

MEASURING CONVERSIONS

Pinch = 1/16

Dash = 1/8 teaspoon or less

3 teaspoons = 1 tablespoon

2 tablespoons = 1/8 cup or 1 ounce

4 tablespoons = 1/4 cup

5 1/3 tablespoons = 1/3 cup

8 tablespoons = 1/2 cup

16 tablespoons = 1 cup

1 cup = 8 fluid ounces

2 cups = 1 pint = 16 fluid ounces

4 cups = 2 pints = 1 quart = 32 fluid ounces

2 quarts = 1/2 gallon = 1.89 liters

4 quarts = 1 gallon

1 oz. = 28.35 grams

1 liter = 1.06 quarts

c. = cup

T. = tablespoon

t. = teaspoon

g. = gram or grams

lb. = pound

pt. = pint

oz = ounce

qt. = quart

INGREDIENT SUBSTITUTIONS

1 cup all-purpose flour - 1/2 cup all-purpose flour + 1/2 cup whole wheat flour

1 cup all-purpose flour - 1 cup + 2 Tbsp. cake flour

1 cup cake flour - 7/8 cup (1 cup minus 2 Tbsp.) all-purpose flour + 2 Tbsp. corn starch

1 cup self-rising flour - 1 cup cake or all-purpose flour + 1 1/2 tsp. baking powder + 1/2 tsp. salt

1 cup self-rising cornmeal - 3/4 cup + 3 Tbsp. white or yellow cornmeal+ 1 Tbsp. baking powder + 1/2 tsp. salt

1 pkg. (1/4 oz.) active dry yeast - 2 1/4 tsp. (1/4 oz.) fast-rising yeast or 1 (1/2 oz.) cake compressed yeast

1 tsp. baking powder - 1 tsp. baking soda + 1/2 tsp. cream of tartar

1 cup honey - 1 1/4 cups sugar or 2 cups powdered sugar + 1/4 cup liquid

1 cup whole milk - 1 cup skim milk + 2 Tbsp. melted butter or margarine

1 cup sour cream or crème fraiche - 1 cup 2% or 10% plain Greek-style yogurt

1 Tbsp. cornstarch - 2 Tbsp. all-purpose flour or 4 tsp. quick-cooking tapioca

1 cup packed brown sugar - 1 cup white granulated sugar creamed with 2 Tbsp. molasses

1 ounce unsweetened chocolate - 3 Tbsp. unsweetened cocoa plus 1 Tbsp. shortening

1 large egg - 1 Tbsp. milled flax + 3 Tbsp. water or 1/4 cup soft tofu

This information has been provided by the Home Baking Association, HomeBaking.org

Praise for
The Cultured Chef

Dr. Susan Bartell, Nationally Recognized Psychologist and Author of *Dr. Susan's Fit And Fun Family*

"At its core, *The Cultured Chef* supports one of the most important bonds — a healthy and nurturing relationship between parent and child."

Nancy Baggett, Award-Winning Author of *Simply Sensational Cookies*

"Visually stunning, and carefully and thoughtfully produced, this charming, unusual book opens up children's eyes to an array of the world's cultures and cuisines."

Father Dominic, Television Host of *Breaking Bread*, and Author of *The Breadhead Bible*

"Exposure to world cultures, diversity education, kitchen techniques, folklore, history, the arts — *The Cultured Chef* is an educator's dream come true!"

Jennie Schacht, IACP Award-Nominated Author of *Southern Italian Desserts*

"Seabright and McIntyre's comprehensive exploration of world culture through the universal lens of food is vibrant and inviting."

Pam Atherton, Host of *A Closer Look* Radio

"*The Cultured Chef* takes children around the world through recipes and stories, fostering cultural development and diversity using the global language of food."

Alethea Kontis, NYT Bestselling Author

"Phenomenally cute, phenomenally colorful, and phenomenally educational, *The Cultured Chef* is all around the world FUN."

Charlene Patton, Executive Director of *The Home Baking Association*

"Without leaving home, readers can travel and explore the cuisine of other countries right in their own kitchen with this delightful book."

Author - Nico Seabright is a children's book author working primarily in multicultural content. He loves folktales, local legends and history. He finds his inspiration when he travels around the world, and his passion is in sharing those stories with others. A native of the Pacific Northwest, Nico lives with his husband Mark and their 14-year-old pug Isabella.

Nico Seabright

Photo By: Russell J. Young

Illustrator - Coleen McIntyre graduated from the University of the Arts in Philadelphia with a BFA in Illustration. Proclaiming a love for watercolor, Coleen also incorporates gouache, ink and other mediums if the illustration calls for it. A native of New Jersey, she found the inspiration she needed in the beauty of the Pacific Northwest where she now calls home.

Coleen McIntyre

Photo By: Russell J. Young

16783787R00159